Why Lincoln Chose War
and how he ran his war
Author's edition

Spencer Gantt

Books and Video Zinc
Publishers

Anyone may quote any portion of this book, *Why Lincoln Chose War,* excluding footnotes and endnotes, per the Fair Use Doctrine, Section 107 of the Copyright Law, provided full credit, recognition and source are given to the author, publisher and printer of *Why Lincoln Chose War.*

Cover design: © Hill Company, Columbia, SC (http://be.net//TimHill)

Cover photo: *A Harvest of Death; Union Soldiers, Gettysburg,* 1863, Library of Congress

ISBN: 978-1468039085

This book is dedicated to my great-great-ancestors who served and fought and died in the defense of their homeland and their families.

Earle Gantt, Sgt
1st South Carolina Infantry
1845 – 1865c

Asa Bowers, Pvt
24th Georgia Infantry
1818 – 1862

John Bowers, Sgt
24th Georgia Infantry
1844 - 1864

Their memories e'er shall remain for us,
And their names, bright names, without stain for us;
The glory they won shall not wane for us.
In legend and lay
Our heroes in Gray
Shall **forever** live over again for us. (emphasis mine)

*Dedication poem for a Confederate Cemetery
in northeast Georgia, 1996.*

BY SPENCER GANTT

VOTE THE BASTARDS OUT!
Democrats, Republicans, Incumbents

SLAVERY AND LINCOLN'S WAR
unnecessary, unconstitutional, uncivil … aftermath

www.spencergantt.com

Contents

Introduction

This book came about as a result of a conversation with my brother-in-law who after reading *Slavery and Lincoln's War* asked me if I was going to write any more books. I said "maybe." To which he replied, "Well, I hope you write a lot more about Lincoln."

There were only a few pages about Lincoln in the first book, but they were definitely not of the "status quo". The facts revealed were somewhat contrary to what we have all been "spoon fed" in most history classes. So, I began to look deeper into the war and its causes and effects and what type of activities and events were going on, not just the "standard pap" we are taught in government schools. A lot has been left out.

Today's "politically correct" crowd would have us believe that slavery was the one and only cause, effect and result of Lincoln's war and that we are to believe nothing else. But, there were so very many causes, so many reasons, so many results and so much going on nationwide that it is virtually impossible to narrow it all down to just "one cause." In so doing, we run the risk of casting aside or ignoring other abundant historical facts to instead pick and choose only those facts and events which fit our own narrow minded purposes.

Today's preeminent historians (by their definition) hammer away at "slavery the only reason" and "Lincoln the Divine" theories. In order to sell their theories they ignore a great many historical facts. They lament that no matter how much they "hammer the public" with their slavery theory, the public still feels that other factors were causes of Lincoln's War, also. Other factors were states (and people's) rights; Northern aggression; high tariffs; incompetent politicians; industrial versus agrarian economies; and, many others. What most people rebel against is the attitude that slavery was the one and only cause of Lincoln's War.

Many, if not most, blame the South for slavery, yet are ignorant of the fact that it was a "national institution" until it became a "political football." If one is going to blame the South and complain of Southern slavery of 150 years ago, then one should blame each and every person, region and country that participated in the institution all the way back to the first days of the 1600s. If you think Southern plantation owners were evil for buying slaves, then what do you think of the people who *sold fifty million* Africans into slavery? What do you think of the people who dragged the Africans through the infamous Middle Passage to North America and elsewhere? Was the first act of war in 1861 the Confederates firing on Fort Sumter, or was it the Unionists sending war fleets and armed soldiers to Fort Sumter and Fort Pickens? We should not pick and choose from history just those facts which suit our own personal agenda. We should look at *all* the facts and make reasoned judgments accordingly. To me, history is five facts. They are "what, when, where, who and who said. *"Real historians"* (so-called) will add how and, particularly, why. And, they are *"real historians"* simply because they tell you they are and you should believe whatever they say. Somehow they know what others were thinking decades and centuries ago just by reading what they said. For myself, I can't blindly accept their interpretations just because they have a lot of fancy letters behind their names, and they are a "fellow" here and have an "endowed chair" there. I can read and I can think for myself quite well. I'm sure you can also. So, as you read my book, collect and absorb all the facts and then you decide ... for yourself ... just what was the cause of Lincoln's war. Maybe there was more than one.

Politics

Lincoln seems to have wandered onto the political scene in the early 1800s. He was somewhat successful at the state level and was elected to the Illinois legislature several times. But, his big desire was to be a national politician. Though it took him a while, we know he reached his ultimate goal in 1860. He served as US Representative from Illinois, 1847 - 1849. This was during the time of President James Polk's Mexican-American war which Lincoln very much opposed as being "unnecessary and unconstitutional." He offered to the House on December 22, 1847, his "spot resolutions" requesting that Polk provide Congress with the exact location (the spot) where American blood was spilled by the Mexicans on US soil, thereby causing a war. Most simply ignored and laughed at him and all he got from the encounter was the nickname "Spotty Lincoln." A resolution was passed by the Whig Party in the House in January, 1848, stating that the war was begun by Polk who sent troops to Texas and Mexico on his own initiative.

In a letter to his friend and law-partner, William Herndon, Lincoln said,

Allow the President to invade a neighboring country whenever he shall deem it necessary to repel an invasion, and you allow him to do so whenever he shall choose.

He felt strongly that the Constitution allowed only the Congress the power to declare war, that the Founding Fathers had specifically made this a legislative responsibility so that

no one man should hold the power of bringing the oppression (war) upon us.

Indeed! Where was this regard and respect for said Congressional power in 1861?

Lincoln had essentially "shot himself in the foot" (and elsewhere) politically speaking by opposing Polk and his war. In the next Congressional elections the Whig party dumped Lincoln and nominated another candidate. But, this candidate lost as well to the Democrat who was a hero of the Mexican-American war.

Considering his political career over, Lincoln dove back into his law practice. He was a very good lawyer, and quite wealthy. He practiced as a corporate lawyer for several railroad companies; even had his own "special car" on some. Once he extracted a $5000 fee from the Illinois Central railroad by suing in court. This was an incredible sum for a single tax case in the 1850s. The vice president of the railroad who paid the fee was none other than George McClellan who became General of the Army of the Potomac in 1862.

Lincoln also managed to do some land speculating while he was a railroad lawyer. It seems he purchased a few plots of land in Council Bluffs, Iowa, of all places. Why this small, frontier town and not Chicago or Springfield? When legislation was passed in July, 1861, which authorized the creation of the taxpayer-subsidized Union Pacific Railroad, guess who got to say in which town it would begin? Why none other than the good president. And, the lucky winner was? Council Bluffs, Iowa.

The siren's call of politics came upon him again, however, and Lincoln ran for a state

Senate seat in the 1854 elections. Because of problems created via the repeal of the Missouri Compromise and implementation of the Kansas-Nebraska Act, the Whig Party had ceased to exist. The Republican Party was born in opposition to these acts. So, Lincoln ran as the candidate of this new Republican Party. Alas, he lost to the Democrat candidate and returned once more to his law practice.

Three years later, the siren was back. The Illinois Republican Party chose Lincoln as their man to beat Democrat Stephen Douglas in the upcoming Senate race. This campaign gave us the Douglas-Lincoln debates which are still famous to this day. But, losing once more to a Democrat politician, Lincoln dropped out of politics altogether feeling he had no chance of ever getting elected to another national office. But, the debates with Douglas, the "Little Giant," had thrust Lincoln onto the national political scene. (Lincoln was 6'4" and Douglas was about 5' nuthin'.) But Douglas was truly a "giant" on the political scene.

Lincoln was an excellent orator which was a huge plus in those days. The more "BS" you could blather about the more you were liked and remembered. During the year 1859 Lincoln was very active in politics in the mid-west making speeches for other Republican candidates, but not running for office himself. In February, 1860, however, he made an appearance in New York City which made him the shining star of the Republican Party. His chances improved considerably with his "Cooper Union speech."

Conventions

Political conventions of the 1800s appear to have been raucous, drunken, wild and roaring meetings of men who had a common cause ... making money through government. Political parties and political power were "all the rage." Deals were cut in smoke-filled rooms, ladies were about, promises were made, delegates were bought. The conventions of 1860 were certainly of this stripe.

The Democrats led off with their convention in Charleston in late April. It was a disaster from the beginning as Southerners mounted a charge against the leading contender, Douglas of Illinois. He was responsible for the Kansas-Nebraska Act of 1854 that allowed the governments of each new territory to decide for slavery or not. This was called "popular sovereignty." It also voided the Missouri Compromise which disallowed slavery above the 36th parallel except for the Missouri territory. Even though the Southerners had voted for this act, Douglas had alienated them by the introduction of his Freeport Doctrine in 1858. This doctrine stated that in any territory which failed to pass laws enforcing slavery, the institution would automatically be disallowed in that territory.

Understand that the truly big issue of the time concerning slavery was the *extension* of the institution into new lands, not its eradication. Had Kansas-Nebraska not been enacted, there would have been no fuss about extending slavery westward, because there were only two territories affected. These were New Mexico and Arizona. Now can't you just see "them old cotton fields back home" popping up all over these two practically desert states? Leave the Missouri Compromise alone and the institution of slavery goes no further west than Texas.

But, Douglas needed a "star in his crown" for his political campaigns and Kansas-Nebraska was it (he thought.) Slave-state versus free-state was always a power struggle for North and South with absolutely no moral concern about the welfare of the black man. Northern politicians, primarily Republicans, wanted slavery ended, yes, but strictly for money and power reasons.

This disaffection with Douglas led to a walkout by the Southerners. Another convention was convened in Baltimore, and a splinter group resulted from that as well. The Democrats "pulled a Lincoln" and shot themselves in their political foot by dividing into three factions. Lincoln would recover from his mistakes; the

Democrats would not.

The Republicans convened in mid-May in the great, new city of Chicago, the center of business and railroad activity in the midwest and beyond. Overwhelming numbers of "delegates" poured into the metropolis where a special hall, the Wigwam, had been built specifically for the event. It held ten thousand people and thousands more were outside politicking (and drinking) in a raucous manner.

In addition to Lincoln, there were several other candidates vying for the nomination including Edward Bates, Simon Cameron, Salmon Chase and William Seward. Lincoln would win the nomination on the third ballot, and his opponents would end up in his Cabinet as Attorney General, and Secretaries of War, Treasury and State, respectively.

Winning over the delegates of the eastern states was crucial to Lincoln's nomination. His campaign managers and staff worked wonders to get these votes. They promised everything they had (and didn't have) to convince the easterners to vote for their man. Lincoln lamented that he could not possibly make good on all the political giveaways and promises made by his crew, but he did. When elected, he paid off each and every promise his staff had made.

1860 Election

Splitting into three factions literally doomed the Democrats from the outset. They had three very good candidates. John Breckenridge of Kentucky was the current Vice-President. Douglas of Illinois was a sitting US Senator with a dozen years of elective office experience. John Bell of Tennessee had fourteen years experience in national office and had been the 16th Speaker of the House. These three men together would poll a million popular votes more than Lincoln, but they would split the Democrat vote "wide open."

Lincoln was probably the most minor of minority presidents ever elected in the States. That is to say, he only received 39%

of the popular vote. He had about 1.8 million votes while the other candidates garnered 2.8 million together. What this says is that 60% of the voting population was against him. But he got 180 electoral votes and needed only 152 to win. And electoral votes are all that matter in a presidential election, unfortunately.

The Founders really did us in with the electoral vote system in the Constitution, Article II, Section 1, paragraph 2 when they almost casually say that "a state may appoint electors as their legislature chooses." Practically all states use that clause to adopt the "winner take all" method for electoral votes. If candidate A receives 50%(+1) of the popular vote and candidate B receives 50%(-1), then A gets ALL of that state's electoral votes. Candidate B gets nothing as his supporters' votes are given to A. Surely there is a better way.

Had a president been elected by popular vote or electoral votes assigned proportionately in 1860, it is entirely possible that the horrors of Lincoln's War could have been avoided. It is doubtful that Lincoln would have mustered a majority in the House.

Slavery

African slavery is the "elephant in the living room" of North American history. In today's world and ever since the early 1800s most people have made the naïve assumption that American slavery only existed in the Southern states. Most are more comfortable with this concept than with looking at the true and total story of slavery, especially if it involved their states, their race or their ancestors. But, it is a known and provable fact that every colony, every state and all the peoples of North America took part in the slave industry in one way or another.

The enslavement of the black race began, where else, in Africa. It continued for centuries and exists there still today. Black natives of various tribes captured and sold their fellow man into slavery as early as the first millennium. The main slave traders at this time were the Arabs. The first "white" people to buy Africans as slaves were the Portuguese beginning in the mid-1400s. Then the Spanish, Dutch and English traders jumped into this extremely lucrative business venture.

In the 17th century the trade cranked up in North America. The first slave ship to sail to Africa from our shores was the *Desire* out of Massachusetts in 1638. From then until the 1860s slave ships from New England and New York transported hundreds of thousands of Africans via the Middle Passage to various and sundry ports in the western hemisphere. Approximately 500,000 captives were brought to North America. Another nine and one-half million were sold elsewhere in the western world, mainly in the Caribbean Islands and Brazil.

The great cities of New York and Boston and their economic prowess were built almost entirely on the slave trade. Rhode Island imported more slaves than the other twelve colonies combined. Narragansett

Plantation was a huge economic endeavor in Rhode Island fueled by the labor of slaves. Great fortunes were made in the slave trade by many prominent New England families such as the Browns, Cabots, DeWolfs, Faneuils, Lodges and Waldos.

The end of northern slavery came in large measure at the end of the American Revolution. Many slaves had fought for the Colonies or the British and payment for service was their freedom. However, this payment went to the slaves' owners as compensation for their ensuing "loss of property." The slaves received nothing, but at least they were free.

When the Constitution was ratified in 1788, it contained four clauses which made slavery a legal institution as it had been for some 175 years or so. All thirteen colonies ratified this document over a period of *two and one-half years*! Eight of these were so-called "free states" and five were so-called "slave states." Why did the "free states" agree to continue slavery when they could easily have ended the system nationwide?

And, why did they "sell their own slaves southward" instead of freeing them?

Lincoln's Views

Many claim that slavery was the sole cause of Lincoln's War and that he brought war upon the States simply to free the black man, and that he was an abolitionist whose only concern in the war was to end slavery. Let's take a look.

Prior to 1854, it's doubtful that Lincoln even mentioned slavery, if at all. This was the year that saw the Republican political party rise from the ashes of the Federalists, the Whigs and the Free Soilers. The "Soilers" sought to confine the Black man to the South so as not to compete with White labor in the territories (ACT105). Certainly, Lincoln never made the statement that his Union army was invading the South to free the black man. Not a shred of evidence exists to show he embraced this doctrine prior to the outbreak of war.

Lincoln made the following statement in the debates with Douglas:

What I insist upon is, that the new Territories be kept free from (slavery) while in the territorial condition. I think we have some interest. I think that as white men we have … Now irrespective of the moral aspect of this question as to whether there is a right or wrong in enslaving a negro, I am still in favor of our new Territories being in such a condition that white men may find a home … I am in favor of this not merely for our own people who are born amongst us, but as an outlet for *free white people* everywhere, the world over (emphasis in original).

In a speech in Springfield on June 26, 1857, Lincoln openly declared himself in favor of racial segregation and the eventual deportation of Blacks back to their native Africa:

A separation of the races is the only perfect preventive, … but as immediate separation is impossible … such separation, if ever affected at all, must be affected by colonization … Let us be brought to believe it is morally right, and at the same time, favorable to, or at least not against, our interest, to transfer the African to his native clime, and we shall find a way to do it, however great the task may be.

More on Lincoln's attitude toward Blacks:

When Southern people tell us they are no more responsible for the origin of slavery than we are, I acknowledge the fact. When it is said the institution exists, and it is very difficult to get rid of in any satisfactory way, I can understand and appreciate the saying. I surely will not blame them for not doing what I should not know how to do myself. If all earthly power were given me, I should not know what to do as to the existing institution. My first impulse would be to free all the slaves, and send them to Liberia, to their own native land.

And more:

I am not nor ever have been in favor of making voters or jurors of negroes nor of qualifying them to hold office, nor to intermarry with white people; and I will say there is a physical difference between the white and the black race which I believe will forever forbid the two races living together on terms of social and political equality. And, inasmuch as they cannot so live, while they do remain together there must be the position of superior and inferior, and I as much as any other man am in favor of having the superior position assigned to the white race.

In response to Douglas in September 1858, Lincoln said:

I am not in favor of negro citizenship ... Now my opinion is that the different States have the power to make a negro a citizen under the *Constitution* of the United States if they choose. If the State of Illinois had that power I should be opposed to the exercise of it.

In his first inaugural address on March 4, 1861, Lincoln made the following statement regarding slavery.

I have no purpose, directly or indirectly, to interfere with the institution of slavery in the States where it exists. I believe I have no lawful right to do so, and I have no inclination to do so.

At Lincoln's direction his Secretary of State had essentially shepherded through the Congress an amendment, the XIII, called the Corwin amendment which read as follows.

No Amendment shall be made to the Constitution which will authorize or give to Congress the power to abolish or interfere, within any state, with the domestic institutions thereof, including that of persons held to labor or service by the laws of said State.

Note the word slave does not exist in the amendment. Nor was the word noted anywhere in the body of the Constitution until December, 1865. This amendment was ratified by two states in 1861, and approved by another convening in Constitutional convention. Of course, Lincoln's war and the withdrawal of seven states from the Union stopped its approval process. But, Lincoln did allude to this amendment in his inaugural address.

I understand a proposed amendment to the Constitution … has passed Congress, to the effect that the Federal Government shall never interfere with the domestic institutions of the States, including that of persons held to service ... holding such a provision to now be implied constitutional law, I have no objection to its being made express and irrevocable.

As for the fugitive slave law, Lincoln referred to it as well stating that it was in essence the law of the land and must be upheld.

There is much controversy about the delivering up of fugitives from service or labor. The clause I now read is as plainly written in the Constitution as any other of its provisions:

No person held to service or labor in one State, under the laws thereof, escaping into another, shall in consequence of any law or regulation therein be discharged from service or labor, but shall be delivered up on claim of the party to whom such service or labor may be due.

I do suggest that it will be much safer for all, both in official and private stations, to conform to and abide by all those acts which stand unrepealed than to violate any of them trusting to find impunity in having them held to be unconstitutional.

In 1862, just before delivering the final draft of the *Emancipation Proclamation*, Lincoln called to the Executive Mansion a delegation of free blacks to whom he said:

You and we are different races. We have between us a broader difference than exists between almost any other two races. Whether it is right or wrong I need not discuss, but this physical difference is a great disadvantage to us both, as

I think your race suffers very greatly, many of them by living among us, while ours suffers from your presence. In a word we suffer on each side. If this be admitted, it affords a reason at least why we should be separated.

You are freemen, I suppose … but even when you cease to be slaves, you are yet far removed from being placed on an equality with the white race. You are cut off from many of the advantages which the other race enjoys …

See our present condition – the country engaged in war – and then consider what we know to be the truth. But for your race among us there could not be war, although many men engaged on either side do not care for you one way or the other … It is better for us both therefore to be separated.

In none of the above passages did Lincoln make any reference to "fighting a war to end slavery" nor did he express any great love for the black race. And he continued this stance and attitude throughout the entire war.

Taxes

Plainly and simply put, taxes are the lifeblood of a government. No taxes, no spending, no government. The early American government was no different than any other world government of the time, and especially, no different than the one from which they had seceded, Great Britain. At the "Boston Tea Party," the colonists had been incensed about King George's tax on tea and dumped it all in the harbor. Then they fought a war to be rid of the King's control and started their own government. And, what was the very first action their new government took? Why, it was to assess taxes, of course, even greater than anything "ol' George" had ever put on them.

Under the Articles of Confederation (which really weren't so bad), the new country hobbled along yet still managed to do well enough. There was no President and it took 100% agreement to pass a revenue bill. But some of the "powers that be" wanted a bigger, more powerful, more centralized government so they called a convention "just to amend" the Articles and strengthen them a bit. But a funny thing happened on the way to Philadelphia and those amendments. The Articles got trashed. Cast aside. Finis. And a whole new governing document came about called the Constitution which we all "worship" to this day. Totally illegal, in my opinion, but that's another story.

The Constitution, while a great governing document so long as it is correctly used and obeyed, had (and still has) many flaws. The greatest of these was pointed out by George Mason of Virginia wherein only a simple majority was required to pass revenue, money and tax bills. Think about it. From the very beginning Northern states outnumbered Southern states by eight to five, and they would NEVER lose that majority; it would only increase. In the Senate that would be a 16 to 10 vote from the "get-go", and we all know that the Northern population increased dramatically every year giving them a permanent majority in the House. A simple majority can lead to a "tyranny of the majority" as noted by John C. Calhoun:

The Constitution will be viewed by the majority ... as shackles on their power. To them it will have no value as the means of protection. As a majority they require none. Their number and strength, and not the Constitution, are their protection.

This all came to a serious head in the 1850s. Since 1788 the South had been successfully and legally fighting Northern domination and control of the government. Most of the first 15 presidents were from the South. A coalition of Southern and Northern Democrats managed a tenuous majority in the Senate, and there were allies in the House as well. The South pumped a huge amount of money into the government via their tremendous agricultural economy. They were an agrarian nation which produced great output in exports and subsequently bought large amounts of imports. All of these exports and imports were taxed by the national government via the tariff.

The problem was that these taxes (tariffs) were neither collected equally nor dispersed equally as required by the Constitution. The South paid about 75% of the taxes to the federal government, and the North spent about 75% of the taxes in the North! The South feared this economic exploitation would only get worse with Lincoln as president.

Lincoln and his party did not care about the sectional imbalance in government nor tariffs, because they were now "on top".

They were not a majority, but they did have power, and the majority would come soon enough. The Morrill tariff was passed by Congress and signed into law by President James Buchanan just days before Lincoln's inauguration on March 4, 1861. This tariff was a "death blow" to the South. They would not submit to what they considered an extreme tax, so seven southern states seceded from December 20, 1860 to February 1, 1861, as was their right under Amendments 9 & 10.

Secession

No one outside the South believed that any southern state would actually secede, least of all, Lincoln. The South had been threatening secession for last 30 years as the New England states had done for the previous 30 years. Therefore, most people at the North didn't think secession would happen.

Secession became a great "sticking point" regarding Lincoln's war. Was it constitutional? Was it allowed? It had certainly been threatened enough though none had actually gone and done it. The threats to secede were basically ignored and taken as the "tantrums" of whichever section of the country was claiming victim status at the time. But, Lincoln said secession was not allowed and he would do whatever it took to prevent it. He was adamant that the South would not be allowed to secede.

Regardless of Lincoln's view, Amendments 9 & 10 to the Constitution state by silence that secession is a right of the states and/or the people. Understand that without these two amendments and eight others known as the Bill of Rights, the Constitution would never have been ratified. Without these amendments the document was, quite simply, a "dead duck." As written, there were not nine states willing to vote for its approval and institution. So what do these amendments say?

Amendment 9 states that "the enumeration in the Constitution of certain rights shall not be construed to deny or disparage others retained by the people." In "Joe Sixpak language" this means that the people have rights not listed in this venerable document. That is, just because the Constitution does not state a right of the people such as secession, this does not mean they do not have that right.

Amendment 10 states that "the powers not delegated to the United States (government) by the Constitution, nor prohibited by it to the States, are reserved to the States respectively, or to the people." Once again, "for Joe", this means that any power or right not given to the federal government by the Constitution, and not specifically denied to the States by the Constitution is a power or a right which "belongs to the States or to The People!" Do you see secession mentioned anywhere in the Constitution or in any amendment? Anywhere?

Power

Some men lust after women. Some lust

after money. Some after power. Some lust after all three. But, perhaps, the most dangerous are those who lust after power. Because, when they get it, they can become very dangerous. Such was the case in 1861.

The Republican Party had formed in 1854, as previously noted, as a "pack of leftovers" from old, defunct political parties. But, the new party was strong and they all had a common desire "to be in charge".

The South had held the Northern states "in check" politically for some 70 years by virtue of the Constitution and the partnership of like-minded citizens in the North. They were always a minority, but managed a governing coalition with Democrats throughout almost all the states. Struggling to obtain control, the Republicans finally made it to the top in 1860 with the election of Lincoln. They were still a minority in the House and Senate, but they controlled practically all the state legislatures and governorships.

Lincoln was elected strictly by Northern

votes, and the South saw this as doomsday for them with higher and higher protective tariffs (taxes) coming their way as stated in the Republican Party platform in 1860. And, so, they pulled out. Initially, this was alright with most of the northern states, and alright with the 75% (and more) of the populace who did not want war.

Striving for Peace

From South Carolina's departure on December 20, 1860 to about mid-March, 1961, there was very little opposition to the secession of the seven states except from Lincoln and some of his cohorts. Politicians, businessmen, private citizens and newspapers were mostly in favor of a peaceful departure. In the *Boston Daily Advertiser* on January 1, 1861, the following was written:

The people desire no war; no attack upon South Carolina; nor do they wish to see her needlessly supplied with any pretext for the beginning of hostilities. They wish only for a *fair defensive policy* in the disaffected State, and for the active influence of the government to be directed against secession in any States that are endangered. And, even now, the distinct adoption of such policy would enable Mr. Buchanan to close his administration with the approval, the support, perhaps we may add, the friendship of his most determined opponents. (OTL405)

One Mr. Everett of Massachusetts, a strong supporter of peace said to a multitude of supporters in Boston:

The crisis is one of greater danger and importance than has ever before existed … to expect to hold fifteen States in the Union by force is preposterous. The idea of a civil war, accompanied as it would be by a servile insurrection, is too monstrous to be entertained for a moment. If our sister States must leave us, in the name of Heaven let them go in peace! (OTL431)

On February 25, 1861, Jefferson Davis appointed three men to serve as commissioners of peace in resolving all differences between the Confederate States and the Union States. The Confederacy had no desire for war. They only wanted what they felt was justly theirs and were willing to pay the Union government for it. They also offered to pay their share of the current national debt so that the North would not be left "holding the bag", so to speak.

The commissioners reported to Washington on March 5 with the goal of speaking to Lincoln to resolve their differences and to acquire diplomatic recognition of their government. Lincoln refused even to talk with them and certainly would not recognize the Confederacy as a separate government or an independent nation.

He had said in his inaugural address that he considered the Union to be unbroken. Therefore, the seceded states were still in the Union in his opinion. If so, why did he not at least talk to the commissioners on this basis, as US citizen to US citizen? He certainly was willing to talk to Governor Pickens of South Carolina throughout the entire Fort Sumter crisis up until April 7.

The Commissioners did, however, speak to the Secretary of State, William Seward. He was considered the "number two man" in the government according to most. He had been a candidate for the Republican nomination in 1860 and received his "plum job" for losing out to Lincoln.

Two former Supreme Court justices were brought in to act as intermediaries between the Commissioners and Seward. They were Justice Campbell of Alabama, an opponent of secession, and Justice Nelson of New York, a personal friend of Seward. Their intent in taking these positions was to assure a peaceful settlement between the Confederacy and the Union. Both were ardent peace-seekers.

The major point of contention, of course, was the status of Fort Sumter and Fort Pickens, the latter existing under a truce drawn up by the Confederates and the Buchanan administration. This truce was, therefore, binding upon the Lincoln administration. The South wanted both forts evacuated of all Union presence, and negotiations to that effect continued between the two parties for some six weeks.

On April 4, 1861, Seward said to Russell, the London Times correspondent:

It would be contrary to the spirit of the American government to use armed force to subjugate the South. If the people of the South want to stay out of the Union, if they desire independence, let them have it. (FAF160)

And on April 10 he officially wrote C. F.

Adams, Minister to England:

Only a despotic and imperial government can subjugate seceding states. (ibid)

From Horace Greeley of the Tribune, the following statements:

If the cotton states decide that they can do better out of the Union than in it, we insist on letting them go in peace. (FAF164)

The South has as good a right to secede from the Union as the colonies had to secede from Great Britain. I will never stand for coercion for subjugation. It would not be just. (ibid)

Whenever a considerable section of our Union is resolved to go out of the Union, we shall resist all coercive measures to keep them in. We hope never to live in a Republic when one section is pinned to another by bayonets. Those who would rush on carnage to defeat the separation demanded by the popular vote of the Southern people would clearly place themselves in the wrong. (FAF165)

Even General Winfield Scott of the Army felt that to avoid bloodshed and the hardships of war, the Union should simply say to the seceded states:

Wayward sisters, depart in peace. (OTL389)

This attitude prevailed from December 1860 up until about mid-March 1861.

The Crittenden Compromise

Virtually the entire nation was for peace in one fashion or another. Only a very small minority, 10% or 20%, were what we would call "war-mongers". They were the extremist Republicans and the Abolitionists of the North, and the "fire eater" Secessionists of the South. With such a small minority calling for war and a huge majority calling for peace, how could a war have possibly erupted?

One of the first moves for peace was a compromise put forth by Mr. Crittenden of Kentucky. He was an elder statesman of the highest order, well-liked and very much respected. His plan called for several amendments to the Constitution, along with four Congressional resolutions. He urged that his proposal be put before all the people of all the states for a vote.

The main thrust of the compromise was the reinstitution of the Missouri Compromise which would disallow slavery in any new territory north of the latitude 36 degrees, 30 minutes, and would allow slavery south of this line. As noted elsewhere, this involved the territories of Arizona and New Mexico. At the time of the crisis, there were no more than 20 or 30 slaves and/or black people in these two extremely arid territories, and it is very unlikely that any more would have come. So, if this part of the compromise had been enacted, the extension of slavery into the territories was probably finished.

Other features of the compromise appeared to be heavily favored toward the South. The ability of Congress to regulate slavery by law was stricken. Compensation was to be paid to slave owners who lost slaves by way of emancipation or running away. The Fugitive Slave Law was to be modified to make it less objectionable to the North. And, none of the amendments once ratified could ever be changed and Congress could never interfere with slavery in any slave state.

It is difficult to believe that such an amendment would be made which could never be touched again by the amendment process. Surely Article V of the Constitution means what it says in that 2/3 of the States could call for a Constitutional Convention at any time to amend said document. But, the main point to remember here is that many, many Americans were trying very hard to avoid bloodshed.

Senator Douglas of Illinois (Land of Lincoln) said this:

Are we prepared in our hearts for war with our own brethren and kindred? I confess I am not ... I prefer compromise to war. I prefer concession to a dissolution of the Union ... Why not allow the people to pass upon these questions? If the people reject them, theirs will be the responsibility and no harm will have been done by the reference.

I am ready to act with any party, with any individual of any party, who will come to the question with an eye single to the preservation of the country and the Union. I trust we may lay aside all party grievances, party feuds, partisan jealousies, and look to our country and not to our party, in the consequences of our action. (LTCxviii)

Senator Pugh of Ohio said this:

The Crittenden proposition has been indorsed by the almost unanimous vote of the legislatures of Kentucky and Virginia. It has been petitioned for by a larger number of electors of the United States than any proposition that was ever before congress. I believe in my heart, today, that it would carry an overwhelming majority of the people of my state; ay, sir, and

Governor Seymour of New York gave the proposal his endorsement:

Let New York set an example in this respect; let her oppose no barrier, but let her representatives in congress give ready support to any just and honorable settlement. (LTCxix)

Large numbers of citizens in Boston passed a resolution for the "preservation of peace." Many, many newspapers pressed for peace including the Albany *Evening Journal*, the New York *Tribune*, the New York *World*, the New York *Times* and the New York *Herald*.
Petitions appeared from all over the country urging compromise of some fashion, any compromise. From Massachusetts a petition was signed by 22,000 citizens. From Philadelphia 2,000 signatures of avowed Lincoln supporters urged compromise. From New York 40,000 "friends of the Crittenden theory" emerged. The New Jersey legislature informed their Representatives in Washington of their support for the compromise. But, it was all for naught.

In December, 1860, Lincoln had written

from Springfield several letters to the
Republican members of Congress:

- reject any compromise which would extend slavery into
  any territory;
- let there be no compromise on the question of extending
  slavery;
- accept no compromise on any kind of slavery extension.

And so, the Crittenden Compromise was
shot down. The Republican Party (and
Lincoln) "dug in their heels" and refused
to approve any peace effort. Lincoln "stood
like a rock" against compromise. (LTCxxiii)
Their watchword was "don't give an inch,
no compromise, no backing down".
(OTL399) They had been striving to take
control of the federal government for
almost 75 years; first as the Federalist
Party, then as the Whigs and finally as the
Republican Party. The Republicans were
not about to forfeit the power which they
would acquire on Lincoln's inauguration
day by throwing it away on some silly
compromise which just might avert
bloodshed.

Immediately after the Crittenden proposal
was voted down, the state of Virginia was
unwilling to accept defeat. Their legislative

assembly invited every state in the Union to a convention in Washington, DC, on February 4, 1861, where they could try once again "to adjust the present unhappy controversies." (LTCxxix)

The head of the Virginia representation was John Tyler, 10th President of the United States who in the opening address said the following.

Gentlemen, the eyes of the whole country are turned to this assembly in expectation and hope ... I trust that you may prove yourselves worthy of the great occasion ... Your patriotism will surmount the difficulties, however great, if you accomplish one triumph in advance, and that is a triumph over party. And, what is one's party when compared to the task of rescuing one's country from danger? Do that, and one long, loud shout of joy and gladness will resound throughout the land. (ibid)

It is doubtful the Republican delegates thought much of Tyler's plea, but the convention debated the issues nonetheless. A proposal for a constitutional amendment was made with its chief plank being the regulation of slavery in the territories. When voted on the proposal carried by only one vote, which essentially killed it.

All this took place before the inauguration,

but efforts and pleas for peace continued right up to the very day Lincoln's war fleet sailed for Charleston.

The First Inaugural

Lincoln's first inaugural speech was quite an effort of some seven pages or more in handwritten form. In it he discussed many happenings of the day, and how things had come to the state they were in. He defined some issues and made several suggestions and promises (some say threats) as to how the country could get out of the terrible bind it was in.

The very first subject he touched on was slavery of the present day. Lincoln said he had no right to and would not interfere with slavery in any state where it already existed; each state had the full right to order and control its own domestic institutions (slavery); he fully supported the Fugitive Slave law and said his administration would support it as well; he said he had no objection to the proposed

13th amendment on retaining slavery which was at that time beginning its way through the ratification process. If the sole reason for secession was to preserve slavery, why did the Southern states not return to the Union as of this speech?

Next up was the definition of the Union and how it could never be "broken." Lincoln said that he "held in contemplation of universal law and of the Constitution the Union of these States is perpetual." That means it lasts forever, right? We know this not to be true. No government has ever lasted forever. Not the Greek Empire, the Roman Empire, the British Empire and not even Hitler's "1,000 year Reich."

He said that "no State upon its own mere motion can lawfully get out of the Union." Well, why not? They got into the Union on their own mere motion, did they not? There was no requirement for *all* colonies to 100% approve any other colony signing in or signing out. None were told before joining that they could never get out or that they would be held in by force, I don't think. But, Lincoln said otherwise.

Regarding the president's responsibility to assure that the laws of the Union be faithfully executed in all the States, consider these powerful words.

In doing this there needs to be no bloodshed or violence, and there shall be none *unless it be forced upon the national authority*. The power confided to me will be used to hold, occupy, and possess the property and places belonging to the Government and to collect the duties and imposts; but beyond what may be necessary for these objects, *there will be no invasion, no using of force against or among the people anywhere*. (emphasis mine)

Some key passages are noted. "There needs be no bloodshed or violence ... no invasion ... no force against the people." Actually, this sounds quite peaceful and accommodating. But, there were other key words as well which were ominous. "Unless forced upon ... hold, occupy and possess ... collect the duties and imposts (taxes)". The Confederate authorities considered this a threat of violent force. Lincoln was saying that he would "occupy and possess" any property that he considered belonging to the Union, and, that he *would* collect the taxes due on exports and imports. These words were considered by many to be a threat of armed invasion and war.

Toward the end of the speech Lincoln said to all his countrymen, "think calmly and well upon this subject … nothing valuable can be lost by taking time … there still is no single good reason for precipitate action … the Government will not assail you." All of it was so very true. Yes, there was plenty of time to deliberate. It was only March 4, the first day of his administration. Peaceful efforts could be made to resolve the crisis. Were they?

He closed with a direct "shot" at the South.

In your hands, my dissatisfied fellow-countrymen, and not in mine, is the momentous issue of civil war. You can have no conflict without being yourselves the aggressors.

In the next 38 days, was there the first glimmer of aggression from the South?

Resupply or Reinforce Sumter?

The *Star of the West* fiasco was an attempt to reinforce Sumter militarily under the guise of peaceful provisioning with some

300 federal troops hidden below decks. A warning shot was fired across her bow and all gun batteries were then trained on the ship itself. The captain wisely turned his vessel about and headed back to sea. South Carolina then stated emphatically that any unauthorized ship attempting to enter Charleston harbor would be fired on without fail. This policy was instituted in January, 1861, and did not change.

On March 15 Lincoln asked each of his cabinet members to give him a written opinion regarding the following question: "Assuming it to be possible to now provision Fort Sumter, under all the circumstances is it wise to attempt it?" The overwhelming majority opinion was a definite "no."

Secretary of War Cameron advised against it. He said

… it cannot now be done without the sacrifice of life and treasure, not at all commensurate with the object to be attained; and as the abandonment of the fort in a few weeks … appears to be an inevitable necessity, it seems to me that the sooner it is done the better. (LTC171)

In other words, he felt it was not

worthwhile to try to supply (or retake) the fort as it would cost too much in lives and money, and the fort was to be abandoned soon anyhow. This was "common knowledge" to the general public and was printed thusly in many newspapers, North and South.

General Scott felt that evacuating Fort Sumter and Fort Pickens (Pensacola) would be a wise move which would impress the eight "slave states" still in the Union and cause them to stay. Such a move might even give South Carolina and Florida a reason to return to the Union as well. (LTC172) Sending a fleet of ships and troops disguised as a "provisioning fleet" to Charleston would be suicidal in Scott's opinion. Such a plan had been proposed by one G. V. Fox, a retired Navy officer, soon to become Assistant Secretary of the Navy. The General said,

An abandonment of the fort in a few weeks, sooner or later, would appear, therefore, to be a sure necessity, and if so, the sooner the more graceful on the part of the Government. (LTC173)

Not only was Scott against any effort of force to relieve Sumter, so was Chief of

Engineers, General Totten, and the entire staff of officers inside the fort. One cabinet member felt the large majority opinion of the general public was for giving up the fort. Another said the risks far outweighed any possible gain in the situation. Another said to relieve the fort would provoke actual combat and civil war. Plus, Fort Sumter was of no practical value to the Union government.

One would think that with such overwhelming opposition to reinforcement and supplying that Lincoln would not pursue the issue further, but seek a peaceful resolution to the crisis. After all, he was a "man of peace", was he not?

The Cabinet Meeting

On March 29, 1861, another cabinet meeting was held, this one being an actual "sit-down and talk" face-to-face type rather than written opinions being solicited. In two short weeks, the cabinet completely reversed its stand on reinforcement from "no" to "yes". This time only two members, Seward and Caleb Smith, voted for evacuation of Fort Sumter. Why the change?

The day before this meeting Lincoln had told Fox that his plan to invade Fort Sumter would be carried out. Immediately after the meeting he ordered Fox to have his expedition ready to sail no later than April 6. He also issued secret executive orders for troops to be assembled and warships to be made ready. What caused this sudden change in attitude about and preparations for war at the North? (RTP 251)

On March 10 the Confederate States had enacted their own Constitution. It was practically a duplicate of the Founder's Constitution except for a few pertinent points. One in particular was the tariff. The Confederate tariff was *only* 10%. What they in effect had done was to create an international "free trade zone" from the Chesapeake Bay all the way to Brownsville, Texas. And, from the gulf port of New Orleans all the way up the Mississippi River to the mid-western states. The 10%

tariff would strongly draw customers away from the Northern tariff of 40% - 50%. This was a virtual "death blow" to northern commerce.

Once this became known, the northern press and business interests turned completely against the South and secession.

The New York *Evening Post* March 12.

... either the (federal) revenue from duties must be collected in the ports of the rebel states, or the ports must be closed to importations from abroad ... If neither of these things be done, our revenue laws are substantially repealed; the sources which supply our treasury will be dried up; we shall have no money to carry on the government; the nation will become bankrupt before the next crop of corn is ripe ... Allow railroad iron to be entered at Savannah with the low duty of ten percent, which is all that the Southern Confederacy think of laying on imported goods, and not an ounce more would be imported at New York; the railways would be supplied from the southern ports.

What, then, is left for our government? Shall we let the seceding states repeal the revenue laws for the whole Union in this manner? Or will the government choose to consider all foreign commerce destined for these ports where we have no custom-houses and no collectors, as contraband, and stop it? ... Or will the president call a special session of Congress to do what the last unwisely failed to do – to abolish all ports of entry in the seceding states?

The *Philadelphia Press* on March 18

demanded a war by calling for a blockade of all Southern ports. This same paper on January 15 had been against military action saying the South should be allowed to go in peace. But this was before the Northern tariff of minimum 40% and the Southern tariff of 10% had been passed. (RTP253)

The New York Times said on March 22 and 23:

At once shut up every Southern port, destroy its commerce, and bring utter ruin on the Confederate states … A state of war would almost be preferable to the passive action the government had been following. (ibid)

And from the *Boston Transcript*, March 18:

The difference is so great between the tariff of the Union and that of the Confederate States that the entire Northwest must find it to their advantage to purchase their imported goods at New Orleans rather than New York. In addition to this, the manufacturing interests of the country will suffer from the increased importation resulting from low duties … the government would be false to its obligations if this state of things were not provided against.

And so, does it appear that the "love of money" came into play when deciding on whether or not to "resupply" Fort Sumter?

A Starving Garrison

We've all heard the story of Major Anderson and his men being cooped up in Fort Sumter and running out of food and supplies. This terrible news came in a letter which had been received by Buchanan a week or so before the inauguration and was simply passed on to Lincoln without action or recommendation. This is how the letter was addressed by Ms. Ida Tarbell in her book.

Almost the first thing brought to his (Lincoln's) attention on the morning of his first full day in office was a letter from Major Anderson, the officer in command of Fort Sumter, saying that he had but a week's provisions, and that if the place was to be reinforced so that it could be held, it would take 20,000 good and well-disciplined men to do it … What was to be done? *The garrison must not be allowed to starve."*

Bad luck this was as there were only about 16,000 men in the entire Federal military at this time; army, navy and otherwise with 90% being stationed west of the Mississippi.

Secretary of the Navy, Gideon Welles, contributed to this scenario as well. In his personal diary he confided that General Scott had told him, Holt and Totten of certain intelligence of a distressing character from Major Anderson at Fort Sumter, stating that his supplies were almost exhausted, *that he could get no provisions in Charleston*, and that he with his small command would be wholly destitute in about six weeks.

Another writer, John T. Morse, addressed the situation this way:

They were shut up in a fort together a certain number of men and *a certain quantity of biscuit and of pork*, which the men would probably eat in about four weeks, then they would have to go away. The problem thus became direct, simple, and urgent.

Let's see. *Starve* in one week, *destitute* in six weeks and *urgent* in four weeks. Not much consistency here. And none of these accounts square with the *Official Records of the Army and Navy of the Union and the Confederacy.*

If you had been a northern, pro-Union citizen at that time, would this not have upset you mightily? Would not the northern press have jumped all over this and begun a campaign against the South for despicably "starving out" the brave little garrison in Fort Sumter? Surely a demand would have come forth for the South to "feed those men or else!" But, nothing was printed to that effect until just before April 12. Why not?

Anderson had moved his men under dark of night into Fort Sumter, an island fortress. No one seems to comprehend that he simply moved his men from one island fortress, Fort Moultrie on Sullivan's Island, to another. He was, therefore, in no worse a position as regards receiving supplies at Sumter than he had been at Moultrie. He had been getting supplies at Moultrie in this manner for months and would continue to do so at Sumter, one would think. Even though the South Carolina government and troops were mightily upset with him for this move which they considered a reinforcement of Sumter, they continued to supply the good Major with foodstuffs, groceries, beef and the like. A time line is in order to determine just who was starving, if anyone.

December 26, 1860. Anderson announced that he had "one year's supply of hospital stores and about four months' supply of provisions" for his command. Three days later he wrote in a letter to Robert N.

Gourdin, a personal friend and prominent citizen of Charleston,

I have supplies of provisions, of all kinds, to last my command about five months, but it would add to our comfort to be enabled to make purchases of fresh meats and so on, and to shop in the city.

January 19, 1861. South Carolina Secretary of War, D. F. Jamison, sent the following message from Governor Pickens to Anderson:

Sir, I am instructed by his Excellency the governor to inform you that he has directed an officer of the State to procure and carry over with your mails each day to Fort Sumter such supplies of fresh meat and vegetables as you may indicate.

Anderson's response:

I have the honor to acknowledge the receipt of your communication of this date ... I confess I am at a loss to understand the latter part of this message, as I have not represented in any quarter that we were in need of such supplies. I am compelled, therefore, with due thanks to his Excellency, respectfully to decline his offer.

Anderson was then given free access to the Charleston markets to purchase provisions at his own discretion. (ACT196)

January 30. Anderson realized that interference from Washington would be a grave mistake and wrote to Adjutant-

General Cooper:

I do hope that no attempt will be made by our friends to throw supplies in; their doing so would do more harm than good.

February 25. J. G. Foster, Captain of Engineers at Fort Sumter wrote to General Totten in Washington that

the health of the command is very good, with no sickness among the officers or men of sufficient importance to take them from a single day's duty. Major Anderson is and has been well, and there is no foundation for the report of his illness.

No mention of starvation.

Excerpts noted hence were stated *after* the alleged "starvation letter" reached Lincoln.

March 8: New York Herald

The War Department today received letters from Major Anderson, the 4th but they contain nothing of especial importance. The most friendly feelings exist between him and the South Carolina authorities. Postal facilities are still open to him, and privileges of marketing, to a limited extent, continue.

March 17. Anderson sent a letter to Jamison in which he said,

I am satisfied with the existing arrangement.

April 1. A report from Anderson showed that his supply department had been selling pork, flour, bread, coffee and sugar to Foster for the subsistence of civilian employees at the fort. These amounted to about 35 days worth of supplies for his command as estimated by one of his officers.

April 3. A letter from Anderson noted that butter and soap had not been included in the day's delivery. Soap?

In late March, orders had been given by Lincoln to fit out the war fleet and make ready for it to sail by April 6. Although these orders and activities had been kept concealed, the secret was bound to out sooner or later. Anderson needed no telling that the Confederates would hardly continue to cooperate in providing supplies for a garrison which within a few days might develop into a menace. When, on April 7, the food supplies from the city were entirely shut off, no one understood better than Anderson that this order was the direct result of news that Washington was about to send warships, troops, arms,

ammunition, and supplies to Fort Sumter.
(LTC187)

Gustavas Vasa Fox

This is probably the most important Union
ex-naval officer of the war that you never
knew existed. Fox was a civilian at the
beginning of Lincoln's war yet "rose" to
the position of Assistant Secretary of the
Navy, due more than likely to his plan for
an attack on Charleston Harbor.

He was the brother-in-law of Montgomery
Blair, Postmaster General under Lincoln
and son-in-law of the father, Frank Blair.
These were two of the greatest "war-
mongers" the North had to offer, equal to
any of the Southern "fire-eaters" in
fierceness and desire for a fight.

Fox's plan was to run a fleet of ships into
Charleston harbor with the pretense of
provisioning the fort, but under cover of
night so that no Union activity could be
detected. He proposed using steamships to

transport troops, munitions and supplies into the harbor. Tugboats would carry whale boats and the first tug would lead in to "draw the fire" of the Confederate defenders. Union soldiers would occupy the whale boats which would be towed into the harbor and to the fort.

In the weeks after the *Star of the West* encounter, the Confederates strengthened their defenses even further with batteries on every available land mass in and around the harbor. Fort Moultrie, which had earned its mettle in the Revolution by routing a British fleet far superior in firepower was "loaded to the gills" with cannon and shot. Castle Pinckney, Fort Johnson, Morris Island and the Battery were all armed and ready to blow away any ship which tried to enter the harbor without permission. From day one the Confederates were capable of reducing Fort Sumter to rubble if they so desired, yet they did not. Why?

Fort Sumter was in a totally vulnerable position. There was no escape and no chance for relief except possibly with a

Union assault from Morris Island. The Southerners were feeding Anderson's troops, so why even try to "relieve" the fort when relief was not needed and such an assault could not possibly be successful? And everyone knew it, especially Lincoln.

One Last Try

Up to this point only seven Southern states had seceded. There were more "slave states" (eight) in the Union than there were out of it. These looked to the greatest of their number for guidance and leadership in this crisis. This was the state of Virginia which had held their Secession Convention in session since February 13. The vote to secede had been defeated as there was great opposition to secession in Virginia. But the leaders held the session open because of concerns as to whether or not coercion (force) might be used against their sister states.

On April 3, Lincoln and Seward decided to send a delegate, A. B. McGruder, to this

Convention to try to get a commitment from Virginia that it would not secede. (RTP258) They also wanted representatives to come to Washington to discuss the matter with Lincoln. The Convention sent a Colonel John Baldwin who was known to be opposed to secession. Baldwin gave an interview to a Rev. R. L. Dabney in 1865 who recorded the happenings of this meeting. (RTP258)

Baldwin reported to Lincoln that Virginia wanted to stay in the Union and that this would help keep the other border states from seceding. The Virginia Convention was not worried about the issue of slavery, but it was worried about Lincoln using force to bring back the seceding states. (RTP259)

The convention wanted a written proclamation of not more than five lines that the Lincoln administration would uphold the Constitution and federal laws. They wanted a firm commitment that he would not use force to bring the states back. If he would sign such a proclamation, then Virginia would not secede and would use its best efforts to bring the seven states back into the Union. (ibid)

Lincoln seemed to be impressed with the sincerity that Virginia wanted to preserve the Union and help bring the seven states back. However, he asked Baldwin,

> But what am I to do in the meantime with those men at Montgomery? Am I to let them go on?

Baldwin answered,

> Yes sir, until they can be peaceably brought back.

To which Lincoln replied,

> And open Charleston, etc., as ports of entry, with their ten-percent tariff? What, then, would become of my tariff?"

Baldwin returned to Virginia with the sad conclusion that Lincoln had probably already decided on coercion. Nonetheless, three other commissioners went to Washington to try and convince the President to use caution and forbearance and to evacuate the forts. Lincoln objected that all goods would then be imported through Charleston and his source of revenue would be dried up. He said,

> If I do that, what would become of my revenue? I might as

well shut up housekeeping at once.

It was very close to the time for the mighty war fleets to sail. Preparations had been ongoing for about a week.

Between a Rock and a Hard Place

This was where Lincoln found himself in late March, early April 1861. He had been elected by a wide variety of different voters and for many different reasons. The slavery issue, the drive for a protective tariff and internal improvements, the promise of free homesteads in the West, and disgust at the split among the Democrats had each played its part. Now with the secession of seven states, the foremost question of the day was whether to let the South go in peace or force them to stay in the Union. The crosscurrents of public opinion were confusing. (LAF269)

As noted previously, there was a strong peace movement in the Northern states. The people saw no need for bloodshed to prove a political point. The border states and Virginia were calling for absolutely "no coercion" against their sister states. And, the Republicans were losing local and state elections left and right. Many voters were beginning to regret they had voted for Lincoln.

But the "men at the top" of the Republican political party had for the first time in 72 years come out solidly on top in the national election. They had Lincoln and that meant they had power, even if they were a minority party at that time. The more aggressive party men among the Republicans, to whom he was under special obligations, were insisting that he exert the full authority of the government even to the extent of war. This group included some of the most active and powerful members of his party whom he could not afford to antagonize. If he pushed for war he would alienate a large portion of the Northern populace and all of the Border States. If he pushed for peace he would alienate the Republican radicals who had put him in power.

On the morning of April 4, the same day as

the Baldwin meeting, Lincoln met with a group of Republican governors, some seven to nine in number. They were from the states of Ohio, Illinois, Maine, Michigan and others. Was their presence in DC all at the same time just a coincidence? All were radicals and "firebrands" so to speak, and all were concerned with the rumors that Lincoln might possibly evacuate the two forts and sue for peace. (LAF275)

Typical of the attitude of the radicals was a letter dated March 27, 1861, from one J. H. Jordan of Cincinnati to Secretary of Treasury Chase wherein he said:

> In the name of God! why not hold the Fort? Will reinforcing & holding it cause the rebels to attack it, and thus bring on "civil war"? What of it? That is just what the government ought to wish to bring about, and ought to do all it can ... to bring about. Let them attack the Fort, if they will ... it will then be them that commence the war. (LAF272)

After the war, Baldwin also told the Rev. Dabney that he had talked with a personal friend of Seward. He asked why Seward had given misleading information about Lincoln's intentions regarding Fort Sumter, and also why he had misled the Confederate peace commissioners concerning the proposed evacuation of the fort. The friend replied that Lincoln had been swayed by Thaddeus Stevens and the radical governors. Seward's friend stated there was "great wrath" shown by these governors and they spoke to Lincoln as follows: (RTP260)

War is precisely the thing we should desire. Our party interests have everything to lose by a peaceable settlement of this trouble and everything to gain by collision. For a generation we have been "the outs"; now we are "the ins" ... now we are the government, and mean to continue so; and our interest is to have a strong and centralized government. It is high time now that the government were revolutionized and consolidated and these irksome "States' rights" wiped out ... we want permanently high tariffs, to make the South tributary to the North ... Our plan should be ... to provoke them to seem to strike the first blow. We shall easily whip them in three months. But this short war will be, if we are wise, our sufficient occasion. We will use it to destroy slavery, and thus permanently cripple the South. And that is the stronghold of all these ideas of 'limited government" and "rights of the people." Crush the South, by abolishing slavery, and we shall have all we want ... a consolidated government, an indefinite party ascendancy, and ability to lay on such tariffs and taxes as we please.

So what was Lincoln to do? If he "let the South go" the government would lose its primary source of revenue. The Confederate tariff of 10% would devastate Northern commerce. The authority of the government and his party would collapse, his administration would be a failure, and he would go down in history as a weak man who had allowed the Union to crumble in his hands. (LAF272) On the other hand he could not appear to have "started a war" just to suit all his "war monger" supporters. He would lose the support of the Northern pacifists as well as the Border States, the Republican party would lose even more elections and, worst of all, he would be a one term president. And, so again, what was the man to do?

Fox to Charleston

Messengers played an extremely important part in the tragedy that was Fort Sumter. The messages they carried, what they said, the precise times at which they were delivered, the purpose and impact of them all contributed to the "attack" on the fort. It began as you remember with Fox taking his military plan to Buchanan and staff in February, 1861. The plan was rejected almost unanimously by the Cabinet and staff, and then again when the Lincoln administration voted it down almost unanimously. But Fox would not give up and early on stated that he felt a visit to the fort (by him, of course) would greatly strengthen the argument in favor of his plan. Really?

Fox got his wish and his visit when General Scott of all people chose him to visit Anderson and "gather" pertinent information as to the feasibility of reinforcing and resupplying Fort Sumter. Scott had denounced the plan as "sheer daredeviltry," but still appointed Fox to go and "evaluate" *his own plan*! This was done with the approval of Lincoln so one wonders who did the actual appointing. Fox arrived in Charleston on March 21.

He had a short visit with Governor Pickens and General Beauregard before being conveyed to Fort Sumter in the company of a Captain Hartstene. Of his meeting with the fort commander, he recalled the following.

Major Anderson seemed to think it was too late to relieve the fort by any other means than by landing an army on Morris Island. He agreed with General Scott that *an entrance from the sea was impossible*; but, as we looked out upon the water from the parapet it seemed very feasible ... I made no arrangements with Major Anderson for reinforcing the fort, *nor did I tell him of my plan.* (emphasis mine.)

Why did Fox not tell the Major of his plan? If an "entrance from the sea was impossible", then why try an entrance from the sea? Virtually everyone alive at the time knew and said that the Confederate defenses in Charleston harbor were virtually impossible to breach. Then why try to do the impossible which could only result in war?

It is important to note that the Chief Surgeon of Fort Sumter, Samuel Crawford, tells in his book, *The Genesis of the Civil War,* of the meeting between Fox and Pickens. He stated that the Governor

understood the object of the visit to the fort to be peaceful, a characterization in which Fox acquiesced.

Lamon to Charleston

Four days later on March 25 another messenger arrived. He was Colonel Ward Lamon, a former law partner and close friend of Lincoln, sent at Lincoln's behest. He introduced himself to Governor Pickens as a confidential agent of the president and declared openly that he had come to arrange for the removal of the command. As in the case with Fox, Pickens was scrupulously careful to extend all courtesy to Lamon, detailing a staff officer to act as escort.

This was great news to the Confederates who had been pushing peacefully for evacuation of the fort for three months. Beauregard immediately sent the news to Confederate Secretary of War Walker in Montgomery. He also corresponded with Anderson who forwarded this same information to Adjutant General Thomas in Washington.

Having been informed that Mr. Lamon, the authorized agent of the President of the United States, advised Governor Pickens, after his interview with you at Fort Sumter, that yourself and command would be transferred to another post in a few days ...

In reference to Lamon's visit, on April 1 Anderson again wrote to Washington.

I have the honor to report that everything is still and quiet … Having been in daily expectation, since the return of Colonel Lamon to Washington, of receiving orders to vacate this post, I have kept these men (workers) here as long as I could; but, now, I am compelled to discharge them.

Anderson then sent another report on April 4.

The remarks made to me by Colonel Lamon, taken in connection with the tenor of newspaper articles, have induced me, as stated in previous communications, to believe that orders would soon be issued for my abandoning this work.

Unfortunately, from Lamon's visit of March 25 forward there had been no evidence of a move toward evacuating Sumter even though he had stated such. This caused Mr. Crawford of the Confederate Peace Commission to telegraph his opinion to Governor Pickens that

Lincoln intended to shift the responsibility upon Major Anderson by the simple expedient of taking no action whatsoever.

The Governor then sent this information to Anderson and also remarked that orders had come from Montgomery to

deny the occupants of the post permission to leave the premises and to withdraw the garrison's privilege of securing supplies in the city." (LTC211)

To say the least, this information must have stunned the Major. On April 5 he sent this communiqué to his own war department.

I have the honor to report everything still and quiet ... I cannot but think that Mr. Crawford has misunderstood what he has heard in Washington, as I cannot think that the Government would abandon, without instructions and without advice, a command which has tried to do all its duty to our country ... What to do with the public property, and where to take my command, are questions to which answers will, I hope, be at once returned. Unless we receive supplies I shall be compelled to stay here without food or to abandon this post very early next week.

The very next day, April 6, Anderson's indignation flared again. Writing to his superiors in Washington he laid bare his poignant dissatisfaction, his mortification at being left alone with his "hands tied" in an inadequately manned and under-equipped fort. (LTC217) Bluntly he set forth his own conclusion,

The truth is that the sooner we are out of this harbor the better.

The notice of Lincoln's intent to send a war fleet to Charleston was written by him and posted over the name of Simon Cameron, Secretary of War. It was sent on April 4, but not received by Anderson until April 7. In part Lincoln said,

> ... the expedition will go forward, and, finding your flag flying, will attempt to provision you, and in case the effort is resisted, will endeavor also to re-enforce you. You will therefore hold out, if possible, till the arrival of the expedition.

When on the seventh Anderson read Lincoln's letter, the shock left him dazed. The next day he mailed another letter to the Adjutant General, the historical significance of which many writers, discreetly or indiscreetly, have overlooked:

> I had the honor to receive by yesterday's mail the letter of the honorable Secretary of War, dated April 4, and confess that what he there states surprises me very greatly, following as it does and contradicting so positively the assurance Mr. Crawford telegraphed he was authorized to make. I trust that this matter will be at once put in a correct light, as a movement made now, *when the South has been erroneously informed that none such will be attempted,* would produce most disastrous results throughout our country ... I ought to have been informed that this expedition was to come. Colonel Lamon's remark convinced me that the idea, merely hinted at to me by Captain Fox, would not be carried out. (emphasis mine)

Talbot and Chew to Charleston

The final piece in this "messenger maze" was Lincoln's sending of these two gentlemen to Charleston. Theodore Talbot was a captain in the Union Army, and B. S. Chew was an official of the state department. They arrived in the evening of April 8. Both were granted an interview with Governor Pickens who requested that General Beauregard be present as well since he was in charge of the defenses of Charleston Harbor.

Lincoln's communiqué which had been received by Anderson the day before was read to them. Both Southerners probably took the message as a "slap in the face" and an ultimatum as well. From "evacuating the fort" to "an attempt to resupply with force if necessary" was a huge turnaround.

Lincoln had given the order on April 6 for the fleet to sail. Immediately the Secretary of War gave to Talbot his orders to proceed to Charleston where, if he found that Fort Sumter had not been evacuated or attacked, he was to seek an interview with Governor Pickens, read to him the statement and give him a copy of it. If he found the fort evacuated or attacked he was to seek no interview but was to return forthwith. The message read:

I am directed by the President of the United States to notify you to expect an attempt will be made to supply Fort Sumter *with provisions only*, and that *if such attempt be not resisted*, no effort to throw in men, arms, or ammunition will be made, without further notice or in case of an attack upon the fort. (emphasis mine) (LAF280)

Let's see. Let's put this into 21st century talk to be sure we understand what the Union representatives actually read.

We are going to bring supply boats into your harbor which you have already told us we can't enter, and if you don't fire at us then we won't attack you with our war fleet which rests outside your harbor and consists of a half dozen or so warships with numerous cannon, and several hundred armed soldiers and sailors onboard.

Is that what they said? Is that what Lincoln actually said?

The message was not only skillfully phrased, it was most carefully timed. News of the preparation of some large expedition had been in the newspapers for a week; but as the destination had not been officially divulged, the writers had guessed at many places, chiefly the coast of Texas and revolutionary Santo Domingo. Not until April 8 did the guessing veer toward Charleston, and the notification to Pickens and Beauregard did not make press until the next day. The first of Captain Fox's vessels were leaving New York Harbor at the very hour that Chew read the notification. (LAF281)

The Fleets Sail

There were actually two fleets which sailed from the North to Charleston and Pensacola. Each was a separate command. The fleet to reinforce Fort Pickens was commanded by an Army officer, Lt. Colonel E. D. Keyes, and the fleet to reinforce Fort Sumter was commanded, as we know, by a civilian, G. V. Fox.

The Keyes fleet was put together beginning

April 4 and it sailed on April 6. Transport ships were the *Atlantic, Illinois,* and *Philadelphia.* They were protected by Union navy ships of war which were at that time stationed in the Gulf of Mexico. The reinforcement had only one hitch when the Navy commander, Captain H. A. Adams, refused to land the troops because of the truce in effect at that time. Once this problem was overcome, the operation was completed with no difficulties.

The expedition to Sumter did not proceed nearly so smoothly. It was put together in the same time frame as the Pickens fleet, and consisted of the steam frigate *Powhatan,* steamers *Pawnee* and *Pocahontas,* and the revenue cutter, *Harriet Lane.* The transport, *Baltic,* was also part of the force. Captain Mercer, USN, was in command of the *Powhatan* and the naval force of the four ships per the following orders from Welles.

The United States Navy steamers *Powhatan, Pawnee, Pocahontas,* and *Harriet Lane* will compose a naval force under your command, to be sent to the vicinity of Charleston Harbor, for the purpose of ... carrying out the objects of an expedition of which the War Department has charge (Scott is supplying the men and material and transports, Fox is to lead them.)

The primary object … is to provision Fort Sumter … Should the authorities at Charleston refuse to permit, or attempt to prevent the vessels from entering … you will protect the transports or boats, open the way for their ingress, and (remove) all obstructions to entry … The expedition has been intrusted (sic) to Captain G. V. Fox, with whom you will put yourself in communication …

You will leave New York with the *Powhatan* in time to be *off Charleston bar*, ten miles distant from and due east of the lighthouse … there to await the arrival of the transports (with Fox on board) … The *Pawnee, Pocahontas,* and *Harriet Lane* will be ordered to join you.

The plan was for the fleet to gather at a specific point off the Charleston coast and take their orders from Captain Mercer on the command ship, the Powhatan. The one flaw was that the Powhatan never showed. It had been "commandeered" by the secret orders of Lincoln dismissing Mercer, appointing a Lieutenant D. D. Porter as "captain" and sending the ship to Pensacola, thereby completely bypassing the Fox expedition. Thus, there was no command ship from which to receive orders.

When the Southerners learned through their sources that a war fleet had sailed on April 8, they had no reason to believe it was not headed directly for Charleston. They considered the sending of the fleet to be an act of war, and they took out Fort Sumter so as not to have to fight the combined fire power of the fort and the fleet.

The *Harriet Lane* was the first ship to appear off the Charleston coast, and broke into the Swash Channel just east of Sullivan's Island where Fort Moultrie is located. At this point the commander of Confederate forces, General Beauregard, ordered the firing on Fort Sumter. No shots were fired by the fleet and no shots were fired at them. In essence, they did nothing to help their comrades inside the fort.

Anderson and his men were essentially pinned down in the fort by the Confederate cannon, though they could return some fire from the lower batteries which had protection via Sumter's thick walls. Anderson signaled with the fort's flag to the fleet for help. The fleet returned the signal, but offered no help.

Fox came in on the *Baltic* and boarded the

Pawnee requesting the ship's captain to move his vessel "into the bar" to help the beleaguered troops in Fort Sumter. The captain refused saying that his standing orders were to await the arrival of the *Powhatan,* the command ship. But, the *Powhatan,* remember, had been sent to Pensacola, so there was no command ship. The captain also stated that he was "not going in there to inaugurate civil war."

Many theories are given for why the fleet did not assist. One is that Lincoln rerouted the Powhatan so the fleet could not possibly proceed into the harbor since they would have no command ship to dispense orders. Another is that the fleet was there only to "draw the fire of the Confederates" and blame them for "starting" a war. Another is that a strong gale was blowing when the assault on Sumter began and the ships could not then enter the fray. (How about the next day?) Captain Abner Doubleday, second-in-command at Sumter, may have been the most correct when he said that "every single Union ship which entered the harbor that day would have been sunk."

Firing continued until the afternoon of the 13th when Anderson surrendered. He and his soldiers were able to leave Fort Sumter with honors and with salutes from their Confederate adversaries. As the steamer, *Isabel*, took the Union soldiers to their fleet for passage home, the Confederate soldiers who had fired on them for some 34 hours lined the beaches on Morris Island, caps in hand, in tribute to the gallant men who had "fought the good fight" against impossible odds yet remained at their posts even when destruction appeared imminent. For the fleet which did not move in to help their comrades in their time of need, the Confederates had nothing but scorn.

Reaction at the North

Several editorials from Northern newspapers are offered here and were written prior to Lincoln's suppression of the press, of course.

The *Buffalo Daily Courier*, April 16.

The news of the fall of Fort Sumter has been received at the North more with astonishment than any other feeling ... If the fort was to be reinforced, why was not the attempt made? ... The affair at Fort Sumter, it seems to us, has been planned as a means by which the war feeling at the North should be intensified, and the administration thus receive popular support for its policy ... If the armament which lay outside the harbor had been designed for the relief of Major Anderson, it certainly would have made a show of fulfilling its mission. But, it seems plain to us that no such design was had. The administration, virtually, to use a homely illustration, stood at Sumter like a boy with a chip on his shoulder, daring his antagonist to knock it off. The Carolinians have knocked off the chip. War is inaugurated, and the design of the administration is accomplished.

The whole country would have supported the President in using force, if need be, to supply the famishing garrison at Fort Sumter with food; but we have no evidence that the Administration attempted this. It might have been impossible for the vessels outside to come to Major Andersn's relief; but we are inclined to the opinion that this was no part of their instructions.

The Providence Daily Post, April 17.

We are to have civil war ... because Abraham Lincoln loves a (the Republican) party better than he loves his country. Ten words from his lips – the simplest assurance that his administration would not attempt to interfere with slavery in the States or in the Territories; and a declaration to the effect that he would rise above party, and attempt the restoration of the Union by conciliation and compromise; would insure a peaceful administration, inspire confidence in the border States, and in a few years at least, bring back the seceded States. Instead of this, he clings to his party creed, and allows the nation to drift into the whirlpool of destruction.

We are told ... that war results ... from an act of humanity on the part of the government – that the garrison at Fort Sumter needs food ... that is all. Is it all? For three weeks the administration newspapers have been assuring us that Fort Sumter would be abandoned ... that to abandon it would certainly disappoint and embarrass the secessionist and kill the spirit of secession in all the border slave States. They had got the public mind all ready for the event, when – presto! – the tables are turned and Fort Sumter is to be provisioned! Secession is not to be killed! Why? We think the reader will perceive why. Mr. Lincoln saw an opportunity to inaugurate civil war without appearing in the character of an aggressor.

There can be no doubt that he intended, two weeks ago, to abandon Sumter. But the pressure from the abolitionists of the North and West was too strong for him. They have forced him to retain a fortification of no value whatever, because to give it up might seem like yielding something to the South. The real motive of a majority of them undoubtedly has been, to inaugurate civil war by what can be presented to the world as an act of peace – the mere feeding of a starving garrison.

The Jersey City American Standard. April 12

The blind or mad politicians in whose hands are entrusted the administration of our government have at length determined ... to initiate war upon our countrymen of the South. There is a madness and a ruthlessness in the course which is attributed to the government which is astounding. It would seem as if it were bent upon the destruction instead of the preservation of the Union ... as if all wisdom and patriotism had departed from it ... (T)he government seeks to mask its real purpose by pretending that humanity requires them to succor the gallant Major Anderson and his troops ... that an unarmed vessel is to be sent to him with stores and if not permitted peaceably to fulfill its errand it shall be done by force. The measure is a disingenuous feint ... This unarmed vessel ... is a mere decoy to draw the first fire from the people of the South, which act by the pre-determination of the government is to be the pretext for letting loose the horrors of war. It dare not itself fire the first shot or draw the first blood ...

No intelligent man will be deceived ... and, if blood be shed it will be laid where it justly ought to be laid, at the door of an Administration which had not the courage to surrender an abstraction in order to preserve the peace and unity of the country. Here is the record of one ... who destroyed by his weakness the fairest experiment of man in self government that the world ever witnessed.

Such articles and editorials would not be tolerated again for the duration of Lincoln's war.

Orville Browning

Mostly a loner, and not prone to be a part of any crowd, Lincoln kept counsel with himself more than with anyone else. He always wanted to hear what others had to say about any given situation. He listened to every different viewpoint he could regarding any subject. He would "digest" others' thoughts and opinions, and then make his own decision, slowly and privately. Very few ever knew what Lincoln was thinking until he actually divulged his opinions or actions to them. According to those who worked with him or for him, "he was the most secretive – reticent – shut-mouthed man that ever lived." Per another, "I knew the man well; he was the most reticent, secretive man I ever saw or expect to see." (LAF265)

When Senator Douglas of Illinois died shortly after Lincoln's war began, Orville H. Browning was appointed to fill the vacancy. He had been a personal friend of Lincoln for twenty years. He arrived in Washington to take his newly appointed Senate seat and went to see his old friend the evening of July 3, just before the special session of Congress would commence. Browning kept a personal diary, probably unknown to most people and, especially, to Lincoln. He entered the following regarding his conversation with the President that night.

He told me that the very first thing placed in his hands after his inauguration was a letter from Major Anderson announcing the impossibility of defending or relieving Sumter. That he called the cabinet together and consulted General Scott – that Scott concurred with Anderson, and the cabinet, with the exception of Postmaster General Blair were for evacuating the fort, and all the troubles and anxieties of his life had not equaled those which intervened between this time and the fall of Sumter. He himself conceived the idea, and proposed sending supplies, without an attempt to reinforce giving notice of the fact to Governor Pickens of South Carolina. *The plan succeeded. They attacked Sumter – it fell, and thus, did more service than it otherwise could.* (LAF287)

If "the plan" was to "bring food to the starving garrison" then it failed. But, if "the plan" was to provoke the South into firing the first shot, then it succeeded, and this is exactly what Lincoln stated. (RTP277) Plus, we know there was no "starving garrison", at least not according to Major Anderson.

One other story surfaces which indicates that Lincoln may have been thinking exactly as Browning said he did, and comes from the Congressional Record of the 38th Congress. On April 8, 1864, a Democrat congressman from Ohio, Alexander Long, in an anti-administration speech to the House of Representatives stated that when Lincoln first heard the news that the Confederates had opened fire on Fort Sumter, he exclaimed, "I knew they would do it!" (LAF287) The speech so angered the Republicans that they tried to expel Long from the House as a "Southern sympathizer" which was guaranteed to get one "jail time" in those days. But the vote failed, and Long's statement stands as a recorded fact in the official Congressional records.

Lincoln and the Constitution

When Lincoln took office in March of 1861, the United States Treasury was completely bankrupt, the growth of the country's money supply being at a scant 1% after having fallen to a negative 4% in the economic crash of 1857. General Donn Piatt related how a plan was concocted by a New England financier to replenish the depleted Treasury by issuing Coupon Treasury Notes, which drew 7.5 percent semi-annual interest payments, were convertible after three years into six percent 5-20 and 10-40 gold-bearing bonds, and which, by Act of Congress, were exempted from taxation. This national debt would be funded by pledging the property and future labor of the American people. (ACT215)

Lincoln was delighted with this plan. However, when then Secretary of the Treasury Salmon Chase first learned of the scheme, he cautioned, "[T]here is one little obstacle in the way that makes the plan impracticable, and that is the Constitution." When Chase's concerns were relayed to the President, Lincoln responded, "[G]o back to Chase and tell him not to bother himself about the Constitution. Say that I have that sacred instrument here at the White House, and I am guarding it with great care." When Chase would not relent, Lincoln called a conference with him and related the following story:

"Chase... down in Illinois, I was held to be a pretty good lawyer.... This thing reminds me of a story I read in a newspaper the other day. It was of an Italian captain, who run his vessel on a rock and knocked a hole in her bottom. He set his men to pumping, and he went to prayers before a figure of the Virgin in the bow of the ship. The leak gained on them. It looked at last as if the vessel would go down with all on board. The captain, at length, in a fit of rage, at not having his prayers answered, seized the figure of the Virgin and threw it overboard. Suddenly the leak stopped, the water was pumped out, and the vessel got safely into port. When docked for repairs, the statue of the Virgin Mary was found stuck headforemost in the hole.... Chase, I don't intend precisely to throw the Virgin Mary overboard, and by that I mean the Constitution, but I will stick it into the hole if I can." (ACT215)

And, stick it he did.

Beginning three days after the Fort Sumter debacle, Lincoln violated the Constitution in many ways, many times as did the Radical Congress. His first violation was in calling for 75,000 troops of militia from the various states to put down the "insurrection" which he claimed was occurring in the seven seceded states. According to Article I, Section 8 of the Constitution, the Congress was the legal instrument to call the Militia to arms. He imposed a blockade on Southern ports which is an act of war against another nation, and, constitutionally speaking, required a declaration of war by the Congress. He called for volunteers to increase the size of the Army and Navy, but only Congress was authorized by the Constitution to "raise and support armies" and to "provide and maintain a navy." One of his worst acts was to suspend the writ of habeas corpus which was also a power and responsibility granted to the Congress by the Constitution. Not even one syllable of the Constitution should ever be suspended under any circumstances, whatsoever, and any changes must be made solely by the amendment process per Article V of this document.

As a very flimsy justification for calling out 75,000 troops, Lincoln used the Militia Act of 1795. Unfortunately for him, however, there was a 30 day limit on the service of such troops after the beginning of the next Congress. If he called the Congress to emergency session to get involved in the resolution of the present crisis, then his new army of 75,000 would have to be dismissed very quickly. And, so, he called the Congress into emergency session for July 4, 1861, almost three months later. This gave him plenty of time to do as he pleased in taking the nation into war.

When Congress did convene, Lincoln said to them regarding the unconstitutional and illegal acts he had instigated:

These measures, whether strictly legal or not, were ventured upon under what appeared to be a popular demand and public necessity, trusting then as now that Congress would readily ratify them. (ACT211)

That's all a President has to do to start a

war? Say that the public "demanded it"; that it was a "public necessity"? The words of William Pitt are appropriate here.

Necessity is the plea for every infringement of human freedom. It is the argument of tyrants; it is the creed of slaves.

He even gave the Congress a resolution on the above matters for them to approve on their first day back. It reads in part:

Be it Resolved by the Senate and the House of Representatives of the United States in Congress assembled: *that* all the extraordinary acts, proclamations, and orders herein before mentioned be and the same are approved, and declared to be in all respects legal and valid to the same, and with the same effect as if they had been issued and done under the previous and express authority and direction of the Congress of the United States. (ibid)

Presto! All is legal and "constitutional."

In 1832, President Jackson threatened to make war on his home state, South Carolina. Daniel Webster's reaction was this:

The President has no authority to blockade Charleston; the President has no authority to employ military force, till he shall be required to do so by civil authorities. His duty is to cause the laws to be executed. His duty is to support the civil authority.

And the same was true in 1861.

Jeremiah Sullivan Black had been Chief Justice of the Pennsylvania Supreme Court, then Attorney-General and Secretary of State under Buchanan, and reporter to the U. S. Supreme Court from 1861 – 1863. He had this to say about war on and among the States.

Whether Congress has the constitutional right to make war against any state(s) or the President to carry it on is a question for Congress itself to consider. It must be admitted that no such power is expressly given; nor are there any words in the Constitution which imply it. Congress does have the power to call forth the Militia to be used within the limits of a State. But, this power is limited in that it can only be used for one of the following purposes: 1) to execute the laws of the Union by aiding federal officers in the performance of their regular duties; 2) to suppress insurrection against the States only when the State herself shall apply for assistance against her own people; 3) to repel invasion of a State by enemies who come from abroad to assail her in her own territory. All these provisions are to protect the States, not to authorize an attack by one part of the country upon another; to preserve their peace, and not lunge them into civil war.

Our forefathers do not seem to have thought that war was calculated to "form a more perfect union, establish justice, insure domestic tranquility, provide for the common defense, promote the general welfare, and secure the blessings of liberty to ourselves and our posterity." There was undoubtedly a strong and universal conviction among the men who framed and ratified the Constitution that military force would not only be useless but pernicious as a means of holding the States (Union) together. (ACT214)

Lincoln, however, did not see it this way.

Hatred

A necessary ingredient in war, don't you agree? And there was plenty of hatred to go around in the 1860s. It had been building up since the early 1600s when North America had first been populated by British settlers.

As noted in an earlier work the first 150 years of British North American settlement involved the Puritans, Cavaliers, Quakers, indentured servants, Scots-Irish/British, and Africans. Some came because they wanted to; some because they had to; and, some because they were forced to. There was a definite split amongst the groups, socially and economically. The Puritans and the Cavaliers were natural enemies because of the Civil Wars of England. The Quakers were, actually, rather neutral people. And, the other three groups were the lowest on the socio-economic ladder of the day. All these devolved into North and South. And, the hatred grew.

New England was the primary carrier in the slave trade in North America. Massachusetts, Connecticut and, especially, Rhode Island, were the number one carriers of Africans via the infamous "Middle Passage" to the States and to the Caribbean from the early 1600s to the 1860s. And, yet, descendents of these slave traders became the "loudest and most shrieking" of the "abolition NOW!" advocates in the 1800s. They were brilliant in their ability to transfer the "sin" of slavery from themselves and theirs solely to the Southern people in the 1800s. Few then and even less now realize that slavery was a "northern industry" for some 200 years.

When the Constitution came into existence in 1789, there were four clauses in the document which allowed slavery. There were at that time five so-called "slave states" and eight so-called "free states". Breaking down on a free/slave basis, I see a vote of 8 to 5 *against* slavery. And, yet, the vote was 13 to 0 approving the Constitution <u>and</u> slavery! Go figure.

The cry of the northern abolitionist fanatics was that slavery was "a sin" and that all who participated in it were sinners and all should be punished, if not by God then by man (them). They had by this time quit with the slave trade and either sold out as many slaves as they had had in their states, or run them out as best they could.

Unfortunately this seething hatred had worked itself into the fabric of the American political system. To be against slavery was to be a part of a "higher cause". Anyone who did not conform to this belief was 'dirt' under their feet, and a sinner as well.

The Republican Party in 1860 used this hatred to stand against the slave-owners of the South. Abolishing slavery was one of the planks of their Chicago platform which Lincoln stood by when he was elected President. Unfortunately, hatred for the South and for slavery was also manifested in hatred for the Union and for the

Constitution. It does not get any clearer than the words which follow.

Democrat leaders of the North were rallying for a return to "the Union as it was and the Constitution as it is", but the radical Republicans who had installed Lincoln as their political puppet in the Executive office condemned the Constitution (ACT219). Members of Lincoln's Cabinet referred to the document as "the tail of a paper kite" and "the rotten rail of a Virginia abstraction." It was Seward's opinion that "a written constitution is dangerous to those of the North. The South is using it as a shield" (FAF23). Wendell Phillips declared in Boston in May, 1849 that, "We are disunionists … we would get rid of this Union … We confess that we intend to trample underfoot the Constitution of this country. Daniel Webster says "you are a law-abiding people;' that the glory of New England is, "that it is a law-abiding community." *But, I say, we are not a law-abiding community. God be thanked for it.* (ACT219)

Representative Clement Vallandigham of Ohio entered resolutions to the House in January, 1862, which proposed that

(1) the Union as it was must be restored, and maintained, one and indivisible, forever, under the Constitution as it is, the 5th Article, providing for amendments;
(2) that whoever shall propose to extinguish any of the States and establish territorial governments within the same shall be guilty of a high crime against the Constitution and the Union;
(3) and, that anyone who shall attempt to establish a Dictatorship in the United States will be guilty of a high crime against the Constitution and the Union, and Public Liberty.

Needless to say, Mr. Vallandigham's proposals were tabled and voted down 78-50, all votes against being cast by Republicans. We shall learn of his fate for this "discretion" (and many others) later.

Thaddeus Stevens of Pennsylvania (originally Vermont and New Hampshire) was even more specific in his denunciation of "the Union as it was."

This talk of restoring the Union as it was, and under the Constitution as it is, is one of the absurdities which I have heard repeated until I have become sick of it. There are many things which make such an event impossible. *This Union never shall, with my consent, be restored under the Constitution as it is! ...*

The Union as it was, and the Constitution as it is – *God forbid it!* We must conquer the Southern States, and hold them as conquered provinces. (ACT221)

Perhaps you remember that Mr. Stevens played a very significant role in the "reconstruction" of the "conquered provinces" after Lincoln's war.

Reign of Terror

Not "la Terreur" of the French Revolution, but the reign of terror in the Northern States under the rule of Lincoln. History books are full of information of battles in the South, terror and burnings by Sherman and his killers, warring on civilians and general destruction of cities, lands, crops and livestock. But very little is mentioned of the difficulties the Northern citizens experienced during their four years of Lincoln's war with its military despotism, supreme military rule and martial law.

One would think by what we are taught that the Northern states were totally united in their desire to fight the South. But, remember that Lincoln was a "minority" president with 60% of the population against him. This was not to improve much during the war. There was still the "opposition party" in Congress, and many "peace lovers" throughout the land. But, these people soon learned what they were up against.

The North quickly degenerated into a cesspool of political oppression. Anyone who disagreed with the activities and policies of Lincoln and the Republicans was considered "a traitor to the cause", and subject to be slammed into jail. Mobs roamed the streets attacking houses where the "Stars and Stripes" were not displayed, and forcing the residents to hoist up the flag. Those who did not speak in support of the President and his policies were labeled as treasonous and subject to be slammed into prison. Many were.

Several Maryland legislators were arrested so they could not vote to have their state secede (which probably would have happened without the arrests.) All this was possible because Lincoln had suspended "the writ of habeas corpus." Now, military officers could arbitrarily arrest anyone they chose (or Lincoln chose) without the need of a court order or charges being brought against anyone.

Secretary of State Seward made the following statement to the British Minister, Lord Lyons:

> My Lord, I can touch the bell at my right hand and order the arrest of a man in Ohio; I can again touch the bell and order the arrest of a man in New York, and no power on earth save that of the President can release them. Can the Queen of England do as much? (FAF213)

To which the astonished Minister replied:

> No, were she to attempt such an act her head would roll from her shoulders.

The British, you see, had laws they actually obeyed; monarchs, politicians and people alike.

In late 1861, three British subjects were arrested under Lincoln's "rules" and imprisoned at Fort Lafayette. They had refused to take an oath of allegiance to the U. S. Government.

A portion of the British Parliament report

of 10 February 1862 is noted.

Friday last some remarks were made on the case of an Englishman in America who had been taken into custody under the warrant of Mr. Seward. Further information has been received in reference to similar cases, but they were if possible worse than the one earlier mentioned. There were no less than three British subjects who had been for four or five months confined in Lafayette prison, and they had been detained there without any charge of any sort or kind having been made against them.

The state of this prison was very bad. In it were confined twenty-three political prisoners, and two-thirds of them were placed in irons. The prisoners were deprived of the decencies of life, and the water supplied was foul and for some purposes it was salt. (ACT225)

Bear in mind this is not Gestapo Germany or the Gulags of Russia we're talking about. This is the good ol' USA, Lincoln style.

The Emancipation Proclamation was issued in two parts, the first in September, 1862. This brought about a huge wave of dissent and disagreement from the Northern people. This disagreement was so very strong that Lincoln had to issue another proclamation on 24 September in which he stated:

... all persons discouraging volunteer enlistments, resisting militia drafts, or guilty of disloyal practices ... shall be subject to martial law, and liable to trial and punishment by courts-martial or military commission. (ACT226)

Two days later, the office of Provost Marshal General was created within the War Department and given the authority to arrest all those suspected of such "disloyal practices." This in effect created a military police force under Lincoln as Commander-in-Chief and was primarily directed at one class of Americans – the Northern Democrats (Copperheads) who had strenuously opposed Lincoln and his war since day one. (ibid)

The Emancipation Proclamation

On September 22, 1862, Lincoln issued the Emancipation Proclamation which was to take effect in 100 days on January 1, 1863, *if* certain conditions were not met by the seceded states. These conditions stated that if 10% of the adult voting population of any given slave state swore loyalty to the Union, they could form a government, retain their slaves and return to the Union as before. He claimed that he issued the

proclamation

by virtue of the power in me vested as Commander-In-Chief of the Army and Navy of the United States in time of actual armed rebellion against the ... government.

Where, exactly, is this power defined in the Constitution?

That Lincoln's act was a supreme "power grab" was the thought of most Democrats throughout the North. Former Supreme Court Justice Benjamin Curtis criticized the Proclamation as follows.

It must be obvious to the meanest capacity, that if the President of the United States has an implied constitutional right as commander-in-chief ... to disregard any one positive prohibition of the Constitution, or to exercise any one power not delegated ... by the Constitution ... he has the same right ... to disregard each and every provision of the Constitution, and to exercise all power, needful, *in his opinion*, to enable him "best to subdue the enemy."

The Proclamation may have been better received had it been applied equally throughout all the States, Union and Confederate. But, it was to be applied and "enforced" only in those States where the Union *could not enforce it.* Exempt from this new law were the following places:

1) all parishes (counties) and the city of New Orleans in

Louisiana under the control of the Union Army;
2) the new "state" of West Virginia;
3) Union controlled parts of Tennessee;
4) seven counties and the cities of Norfolk and Portsmouth in Virginia;
5) all Northern states including the four slave states of Maryland, Delaware, Kentucky and Missouri.

Exemption of all these places under Union control and, especially, the four slave states prompted the New York World to write:

He has proclaimed emancipation only where he has notoriously no power to execute it. The exemption of the accessible parts of Louisiana, Tennessee, and Virginia renders the proclamation not merely futile, but *ridiculous*. (emphasis mine)

British foreign minister and observer of the war, Earl John Russell, said:

There seems to be no declaration of a principle adverse to slavery in this proclamation. It is a measure of war, and a measure of war of a very questionable kind.

Lincoln himself was reluctant to think that the act would accomplish anything in the way of actual emancipation of any slaves anywhere. Just before the issuance he said:

… what reason is there to think it would have any greater effect upon the slaves than the late law of Congress, which I approved, and which offers protection and freedom to the slaves … who come within our lines? Yet I cannot learn that that law has caused a single slave to come over to us. And suppose they could be induced … to throw themselves upon us, what would we do with them? How can we feed and care for such a multitude? General Butler wrote me a few days since that he was issuing more rations to the slaves who have rushed to him than to all the white troops under his command. They eat, and that is all.

For two years the South, very new and small nation that it was, had been battling "toe to toe" with the vast and mighty Union armies and had come out on top. Through Manassas, Sharpsburg and Fredericksburg as well as others, the Confederates had either scored victories or, at least, pyrrhic victories. Though Lincoln had refused to acknowledge the South as an independent nation, the Southerners had not been idle in seeking recognition from the world's other countries. They had reached the point where England was considering entering the fray to "offer mediation ... with a view to the recognition of the independence of the Confederates." And if mediation failed, England should recognize the South on her own.

This would have been complete disaster for the North. War with the South *and* England was a definite loser. The Emancipation Proclamation, therefore, was designed to give a "great moral purpose" to the war and to cause the non-slave nations of the world (including England) to either side with the North or remain neutral. If the South could be made to appear the "evil perpetrators of slavery" and the North the "saviors of the poor slaves", then the non-slave nations could not possibly side with the Confederacy. It was a brilliant move.

There was one more possible effect which may have been on the mind of the Unionists with the issuance of the Proclamation. For decades the maniacal abolitionists of New England had been calling for the indiscriminate slaughter and murder by the slaves of their masters and, probably, any other white Southerner who happened along. Many suspected that Lincoln had caved in to the pressure of the abolitionists, and issued the Proclamation with the thought that the Southern slaves would rise up in armed and murderous revolt. With mostly women, children and elderly present among overwhelming numbers of slaves a scene not unlike that of the Haiti massacres was possible. The slave revolt in St. Domingo in October, 1791, was definitely on the mind of many.

In an instant twelve hundred coffee and two hundred sugar plantations were in flames ... the unfortunate proprietors hunted down, murdered or thrown into the flames by infuriated negroes ... The unchained African signalized his ingenuity by the discovering of new and unheard-of modes of torture. An unhappy planter was sawed asunder between two boards; the horrors inflicted on the women exceeded anything known even in the annals of Christian ferocity ... Crowds of slaves traversed the country with the heads of white children affixed on their pikes ... In a few instances only, the humanity of the negro character resisted the savage contagion of the time; and some faithful slaves, at the hazard of their own lives, fed in caves their masters or their children, whom they had rescued from destruction.

The Emancipation Proclamation did not free many slaves, if any, but at least it did not produce the murderous "servile insurrection" that many had hoped for. The Southern slaves held to the honor of mankind and achieved their freedom slowly perhaps, but at least in a human and civilized manner.

The Loyal Opposition

Such people have existed in the States forever, I'm sure. No one likes to fight and, certainly no one wants to die ... not for someone else's cause.

Lincoln had his war protesters. He himself had even been a war protester against Polk's war. But, now he had his own war, thank you, and things were different. His solution? Throw 'em in jail. And, by the tens of thousands he did. Since all the Northern states were under martial law and, therefore, Lincoln's rule, it was easy to get hauled off to a military jail and disappear for a while if not forever. Charges and warrants were not necessary, and you could be imprisoned if you just spoke out against Lincoln's war or if you spoke not at all. Silence was as treasonous as a big mouth.

The main group of "loyal opposition" in the North was the Democrat Party. These people were "pro-Union, anti-secession and anti-war." For these attributes they were called "Copperheads" by the Lincolnites likening them to the copperhead snake (in the grass, I suppose.) But, there was nothing "sneaky" about these Peace Democrats. They were very up front and forward about their feelings and ideals. They felt that the problems regarding secession and emancipation should be settled judicially and constitutionally. Emancipation was, indeed, finally realized on 6 December 1865 by constitutional means. Secession, however, was ruled illegal by means of raw, military power ... no Constitution or courts required. But they should have been.

A prominent member of the loyal opposition group was one Clement Vallandigham, a duly elected US Representative of Ohio. He was a Democrat who had the audacity to be against Lincoln's War, and Lincoln's illegal arrests and imprisonments. He never shut up about his beliefs and those of his fellow peace lovers, and he eventually paid for his "treasonous acts."

In the early morning hours of May 2, 1863, armed men surrounded Vallandigham's home in Dayton, Ohio. They broke down the doors and searched the house. Finding the unfortunate Representative asleep, they dragged him out of bed, arrested him and soon he was on his way by train to

Cincinnati for a very speedy military trial. Convicted of treason he was then sent to a federal prison. Lincoln exiled this man to the South where he eventually made his way to Canada. This is the President of the United States having a member of Congress arrested, tried in military court and run out of his country. (FAF210)

Neither was the Church immune from Lincoln's gendarmes. J. R. Stewart, clergyman of Saint Paul's Episcopal Church in Alexandria, Virginia, was arrested on 9 February 1862 by the order of the State Department (Seward) in Washington, D.C. Charges were that Stewart refused to pray for the President, and the congregation had exhibited "habitual mockery of the Stars and Stripes and insolent bearing toward Union citizens and U.S. soldiers." (ACT235)

Soldiers from the Eighth Illinois Cavalry invaded the church, surrounded the minister as he prayed, and shoved sabres at him to speak only as commanded. The priest began his prayer, "From all evil and mischief; from all sedition, privy conspiracy ..." The congregation responded, "Good Lord, deliver us." The officer in charge grabbed the Bible from Stewart's hands and threw it to the ground shouting, "You are a traitor! In the name and by the authority of the President of the United States, I arrest you!" Glory, glory, hallelujah ... huh? (ibid)

The office of the newspaper which reported these atrocities was burned to the ground, as was that of the religious journal, *The Southern Churchman.* Stewart was exiled from his home, and spent the duration of the war ministering to the wounded and dying on the battlefields, and in the prisons and hospitals.

Not to be left aside, the newspapers of the North were ravaged as well during the four long years of Lincoln's War. Hundreds were torched and burned to the ground. Printing presses and subscription lists were destroyed; type-setting and all associated equipment was destroyed. Mobs, many times of ex-soldiers, set upon the publishers and drove them and their families and workers from their homes and towns. Many were tarred and feathered, and ridden out of town on a rail. Some were forced to kneel on the ground in front of the mobs and "confess their sins" and promise they would write nothing more against Lincoln, his war or his military government.

The editorials noted earlier, written after the Fort Sumter battle were decidedly against Lincoln and his actions, as were many when the Militia was illegally called up. These articles ceased in the hot and dangerous "summer of '61" when so many opposition newspapers (Democrats) were destroyed. From thence forward only "positive press" for the government was permitted. To speak out against Lincoln and anything he said, thought or did was a crime, classified as treason.

Not once did Lincoln speak out against the mobs destroying opposition newspapers, or the atrocities committed against the editors and their families He did, however, grant many, many lucrative government positions and contracts to the editors and owners of favorable (Republican) papers.

1864 Election

For most of 1864, re-election prospects for Lincoln did not look good. He himself felt he would lose. No president since Jackson had won re-election, a period of some 30 years. A large number of the Northern public was still angry about his Emancipation Proclamation fearing its impact on American society. And, the war was not going swimmingly. Union defeats in the summer had produced some 65,000 casualties and "missing" whereas the first three years had produced some 110,000. Nor was the Republican Party solidly behind Lincoln. Some in the party began to push for constitutional amendments to abolish slavery and assure racial equality for all. What a great idea to have been pushed in the 1850s and, especially 1860/61 rather than a bloody war to allegedly accomplish these two noble goals.

The Democrats were up to their old tricks

of "divide and lose elections" again. There were Peace Democrats who were for war against the South, but also wanted a negotiated peace. And, there were some who wanted instant peace with no war in hopes that this would achieve a Union victory without totally destroying the South. Then there were the War Democrats who were not much different than the Radical Republicans who wanted total war and the unconditional surrender of the South.

The Republicans were having their own problems with factions though there were apparently no "peace lovers" among them. They suddenly renamed their party "The National Union Party" so as to gather in the War Democrats and any other groups which were intent on total destruction. Also, the title "Republican" may not have been too much in vogue in the North after three and a half years of butchery, bloodshed and an unnecessary war. Lincoln's victory was far from guaranteed.

In October and November elections took place in the principal States, with the results that New York, New Jersey, Pennsylvania, Ohio, Indiana, Illinois, and Wisconsin, all of which except new Jersey had cast their electoral votes for Lincoln, declared against the party in power (Republican). The Democrats made conspicuous gains in the House as a result. A disaster was avoided when the Administration was saved by strong returns from New England, Michigan, Iowa and the Border Slave States. With the election drawing near, Lincoln knew his political career was in serious jeopardy. How he overcame these immense obstacles to secure a second term is indicative of how far removed from a constitutional foundation his Administration had become by late 1864.

A phrase from Francis Lieber about military dictators is well noted here.

The Caesar always exists before the imperatorial government is acknowledged and openly established. Whether the praetorians or legions actually proclaim the Caesar or not, it is always the army that makes him.

The Union army played a huge role in Lincoln's reelection. Just a couple of weeks before the election, thousands were given significant furloughs to return home if they promised to vote for Lincoln and the Republican ticket. And, so, "it is always the army that makes him."

Union soldiers were also used at the polls to assure that no one "disturbed the peace" on election day. One such encounter is noted in New York City where reports (to Lincoln) indicated that the city would give a large majority for the Democrat opponent. The teller of the story is one Benjamin Butler, the Union "general of New Orleans" commonly known as "Beast Butler" for more than obvious reasons.

Hearing of the impending election crisis in New York, Secretary of War Stanton telegraphed General Butler to report to Washington for orders to alleviate the problem. He was sent to New York and Grant was ordered to send him 5,000 troops from the Western theater along with two batteries of Napoleon guns. When the citizens saw the troops and cannon, there was great agitation and uneasiness over the city. Newspapers charged that these warlike preparations were made to overawe citizens and prevent a fair election. Butler denied these accusations yet sent a letter to Stanton the day before the elections which stated:

I beg leave to report that the troops have all arrived and dispositions made which will insure quiet. I enclose copy of my order No. 1, and trust it will meet your approbation. I have done all I could to prevent secessionists from voting, and think it will have some effect.

"Secessionists" would have meant any New York Democrats with the thought of voting for McClellan, the Democrat candidate. Lincoln carried the state of New York by less than 1% of the vote.

"Bayonets at the ballot box" was not a new tactic. It had been used in Maryland in 1861 to intimidate voters into not voting for secession as they surely would have done if allowed to vote without militaristic intimidation. After April, 1865, it was used exclusively in the South until 1877 to assure that newly franchised black citizens voted the Republican ticket. White citizens were not allowed to vote.

Hampton Roads

The Hampton Roads Peace Conference was held on February 3, 1865, on a steam ship near Hampton Roads, Virginia. Mr. Francis P. Blair, Sr., instigated the conference by obtaining President Lincoln's permission to contact Confederate President Jefferson Davis, concerning a possible temporary halt in the war. Mr. Blair was closely connected to the Lincoln administration and he was concerned about the efforts on the part of the French to establish a military presence in Mexico in order to help them reconquer the territory that had been lost in the war with America. He proposed that a secret military conference take place and that all hostility cease between North and South for the purpose of sending an American army to evict the French from Mexico. This would stop any assault by the Mexicans on the southwestern United States. Lincoln gave Blair permission to talk to Davis, but indicated to him that he did not endorse Blair's ideas. However, he would not stand in the way of some military conference to discuss peace terms.

Davis appointed three delegates to the conference. They were Alexander Stephens, Vice –President of the Confederate States; John Campbell, a former Supreme Court Justice from Alabama; and a R. M. T. Hunter who was a member of the Confederate Senate. The delegates were given safe passage through Northern lines and met directly with General Grant, who sent them safely to meet President Lincoln and Secretary of State William Seward.

Mr. Seward said this was to be an informal conference with no writing or record to be made; all was to be verbal and the Confederates agreed.

Lincoln:

The trip of Mr. Blair was approved by me, but I do not endorse the idea to halt the hostilities for the purpose of the American army going to Mexico to enforce the Monroe Doctrine; however, I have no objection to discussing a peace offer at this time. I have always been willing to discuss a peace offer as long as the first condition is met and that would be for the Confederacy to pledge to return to the Union. If that condition would be agreed upon then we could discuss any other details that were necessary.

Stephens:

If we could come up with some proposal to stop the hostilities, which might lead to the restoration of the Union without further bloodshed, would it not be advisable to act on that proposal, even without an absolute pledge of ultimate restoration being required at the beginning?

Lincoln:

There will be no stopping of the military operations unless there is a pledge first by the Confederacy to rejoin the Union immediately.

Campbell:

What would be the terms offered to the South if they were to pledge to rejoin the Union and how would they be taken back into the Union?

No immediate response from Lincoln or Seward.

Stephens:

It would be worthwhile to pursue stopping the hostilities to have a cooling off period so that the peace terms might be investigated without the passions of war. Should the hostilities stop for some extended period of time, I feel that there would be a good chance that many of the states would rejoin the Union on the same terms as they had when they joined in the beginning, but that the sovereignty of the states would have to be recognized upon rejoining the Union.

Seward:

A system of government founded upon secession would not last and self-preservation of the Union is a first law of nature which applies to nations as well as to individuals.

Stephens:

What will be the status of the slave population in the Confederate states, and especially what effect will the Emancipation Proclamation have if the Confederate States rejoin the Union?

Lincoln:

The Proclamation was only a war measure and as soon as the war ceases, it will have no operation for the future. The Courts will decide that the slaves who were emancipated under the Proclamation would remain free but those who were not emancipated during the war would remain in slavery.

Seward:

Only about two hundred thousand (200,000) slaves had come under the operation of the Proclamation. This would be a small number out of the total.

Stephens:

What would be the status of the states in regard to their representation in Congress?

Lincoln:

They would have their full rights restored under the Constitution. There would be no punishment or reconstruction imposed.

Lincoln:

It was never my intention to interfere with slavery in the states where it already existed and I would not have done so during the war, except that it became a military necessity. I have always been in favor of prohibiting the extension of slavery into the territories but never thought immediate emancipation in the states where it already existed was practical. There would be "many evils attending" the immediate ending of slavery in those states.

Hunter:
Your proposals sound like an unconditional surrender.

Seward:
The North would not be conquerors but rather the states would merely have to recognize national authority and the execution of the national laws. The South would regain full protection of the Constitution like the rest of the states.

Lincoln:
I think the North would be willing to be taxed to compensate the Southern people for the loss of their slaves. I have had many conversations to the effect that if there was a voluntary abolition of slavery the American government would pay a fair indemnity and four hundred million dollars ($400,000,000) would probably be appropriated for this purpose.

Seward:
The Northern people are very weary of the war and they would be willing to pay this amount of indemnity rather than continuing to pay for the war.

Mr. Stephens wrote that the entire conversation took about four hours and the last subject was the possible exchange of prisoners. Lincoln stated he would put that question in the hands of General Grant and they could discuss it with him as they left.

Stephens:

Mr. President, would you reconsider stopping the hostilities for a period of time so that the respective sides could "cool off," and while cooling off, investigate further possibilities for ending the war other than by simply having the South pledge to rejoin the Union?

Lincoln:

I will reconsider it but I do not think my mind will change on that point.

Thus ended the Peace Conference and the Confederates returned to meet with General Grant and were escorted back to the Confederate lines.

Note: Grateful appreciation is extended to John V. Denson and Llewelyn Rockwell for allowing me to quote from the article, *The Hampton Roads Peace Conference During the War Between the States,* January 10, 2006. You may read the complete article at Mr. Rockwell's website.

http://www.lewrockwell.com/orig2/denson6.html

War

What is it good for? Absolutely nothing. So went the 1969 anti-war Viet Nam protest song by Edwin Starr. Perhaps he won't mind some of the lyrics here (free on the Internet.)

"war I despise because it means destruction of innocent lives; tears to thousands of mothers eyes when their sons go to fight and lose their lives; it ain't nothing but a heartbreaker, friend only to the undertaker."

Wars are never started by "the people". That's you and me, by the way, and people like us. The people are never asked if they would "like" to go to war, as then there would never be any wars. Can you imagine this scenario?

Sir, would you like to go over to Europe and help our dear allies, the Russian communists, kill the German Nazis? Well, yes, you will probably be killed or, hopefully, just maimed or captured and tortured for a few years.

Madam, would you like to volunteer your sons to go over to Southeast Asia and kill the evil communists so that Viet Nam can be a free, democratic nation? Well, yes, your sons will probably be killed or, hopefully, just maimed or captured and tortured for a few years.

Could you see that happening? Never a chance! "We the people" are never asked, we are simply ordered to fight. Or else. Wars are always started by unscrupulous, egomaniacal so-called "leaders" who are consumed with and driven by a "lust for power" and "a love of money". Someone always gets richer as a result of war, and "it ain't the people." A government at war always gains more power over its citizens who then lose more of their liberties. And, "the people" always die, not the "leaders."

John Denson writes in his book, *A Century of War*, that the twentieth century (1900s) was the bloodiest in all of history. More than 170 million people were killed by governments and a high percentage of these were innocent civilians. That is a staggering statistic of almost two million people killed every year. For what? Absolutely no good reason.

Lincoln's War was the bloodiest in the nineteenth century and the bloodiest in history at that point. And, it was all completely unnecessary as all wars are. There were multiple opportunities for a peaceful resolution of differences between the two regions. Some may not have been ideal, but at least they were peaceful solutions. No murder or rape required. No thievery, burning or destruction. No loss of innocent lives. Is it not better to talk ones way out of differences than to murder ones way out? Is it not better to compromise than to kill? Make one compromise and then work toward a better one.

The seeds of Lincoln's War came to North America as noted previously when the Puritans, Cavaliers, Quakers, indentured servants, Scots-Irish/British and Africans came "boiling into" the continent in the 1600s and 1700s. With them came many types of strife, not the least of which were slavery and religion. The Puritans brought us both of these early on and then used the latter to try and end the first.

The second Great Awakening in New England was a fanatical evangelical religious movement which defined slavery as an "evil and a sin" that must be eradicated. This was the slavery which they had created. The movement infected political thought and action with the notions of "good and evil." It was, perhaps, our first infraction of the Bill of Rights wherein the government made laws and took actions which were dependent upon "good and evil", appealing to a "higher power" for guidance rather than the Constitution. It was our first failure in "separation of church and state."

Lincoln himself even dragged religion into his conflict. After almost four years of "murder, mayhem and extreme bloodshed" he blamed it all on God. In his second inaugural address he said,

He gives to both North and South this terrible war as the woe due to those by whom the offense came ... Fondly do we hope, fervently do we pray, that this mighty scourge of war may speedily pass away. Yet, if God wills that it continue ... so still it must be said "the judgments of the Lord are true and righteous altogether."

God help me, it's all I can do when reading this speech not to throw up, as it is so hypocritical and condescending. God gave both North and South this terrible war? I don't recall that God was at the Hampton Roads conference. I don't recall that God said

There will be no stopping of the military operations unless there is a pledge first by the Confederacy to rejoin the Union immediately.

I don't recall that God sent a war fleet to Charleston to deliver a "boatload of biscuit and pork."

The President, whoever he was or is, from Polk to Obama, is the "man with his finger on the trigger." In our history, wars (or bombings) always start with this one man. He is the one man with the power to act for war ... or for peace. God doesn't bring wars upon us. God is a Prince of Peace.

John Shipley Tilley in his book, *Lincoln Takes Command,* suggests a scenario in which a true leader could have taken command of the situation in April of 1861 by this simple request.

I call upon you to join with me in arranging a conference to be participated in by every state. It is my earnest request that each delegate shall come with one and only one instruction, and that this shall be, "There is to be no war."

Amen, Mr. Tilley.

I close with a quote from our great ancestor, Benjamin Franklin, in 1783.

There was never a good war, or a bad peace.

Recommended Reading

A CENTURY OF WAR Lincoln, Wilson &
 Roosevelt, John V Denson, Ludwig von Mises
Institute, Auburn Alabama, 2006, 2008

AMERICA'S CAESAR the Decline and Fall of
Republican Government in the US (ACT),
Greg Loren Durand, Confederate Reprint Company
Dahlonega Georgia, 2006

FACTS AND FALSEHOODS Concerning the
War on the South 1861 – 1865 (FAF)
George Edmonds, Confederate Reprint Company
Dahlonega Georgia, 2000/1904

FORCED INTO GLORY Abraham Lincoln's
White Dream, Lerone Bennett, Jr.
Johnson Publishing Company, Chicago, 2007

LINCOLN AND FORT SUMTER (LAF)
Charles W. Ramsdell, Southern Historical Association
www.bonniebluepublishing.com 1937

LINCOLN TAKES COMMAND (LTC)
John Shipley Tilley, University of North Carolina Press
Chapel Hill, 1941

LINCOLN UNMASKED What You're Not
Supposed to Know About Dishonest Abe
Thomas J. DiLorenzo, Three Rivers Press, New York,
2006

ORIGIN OF THE LATE WAR (OTL) George
Lunt, Confederate Reprint Company, Dahlonega
Georgia
2003/1866

REASSESSING THE PRESIDENCY The Rise
of the Executive State and the Decline of Freedom
(RTP) John V. Denson Editor, Ludwig von Mises
Institute, Auburn Alabama, 2001

THE REAL LINCOLN A New Look at Lincoln,
His Agenda and an Unnecessary War
Thomas J. DiLorenzo, Three Rivers Press, New York
2002/2003

THE SUNKEN FACT: Lincoln Instigated the War
www.americancivilwar.com, Joe Ryan Original Works
Los Angeles

End Notes

Page Reference

3   George McClellan: *Why the Republican Party Elected Lincoln*, Thomas J. DiLorenzo. www.lewrockwell.com/dilorenzo/ dilorenzo53.html

3   And the lucky winner was: ibid.

15   What I insist upon is: ibid, quoting Lincoln, reply to Douglas on 15 October 1858.

15   A separation of the races: ibid, 106, quoting Lincoln, address at Springfield, Illinois, 26 June 1857.

15   When Southern people tell us: ibid, quoting Lincoln, reply to Douglas at Peoria, Illinois on 16 October 1858.

16   I am not, nor ever have been: ibid, 107 quoting Lincoln, speech delivered at Charleston, Illinois on 18 September 1858.

16   I am not in favor of negro citizenship: ibid, quoting Lincoln, reply to Douglas on 18 September, 1858.

18   You and we are different races: ibid, quoting Lincoln, speech delivered at Executive Mansion on 14 August 1862.

21 The Constitution will be viewed: ibid, 219, Quoting John C. Calhoun letter to James H. Hamilton, 28 August 1832.

46 Evening Post March 12: *Northern Editorials on Secession,* Howard Cecil Perkins Editor, Appleton-Century Company, New York, 1942, 598-601

48 Almost the first thing: *The Life of Abraham Lincoln,* Ida M. Tarbell, McClure/Phillips, New York, 1900, III 14-15

49 Certain intelligence of: ibid quoting *Diary of Gideon Welles,* Riverside Press Cambridge, Boston/New York, 1911, I, 4

49 They were shut up: *Life of Lincoln,* John T. Morse, Houghton-Mifflin, Boston, I 244

50 Four months' supply: *Official Records of the Union and Confederate Armies and Navies War of the Rebellion (ORA/ORN)* ORA, S1, V1, P2

50 Robert N. Gourdin: *The Genesis of the Civil War,* Samuel W. Crawford, C. L. Webster & Co., New York, 1887, 128

51 Sir, I am instructed: ORA, S1, V1, 144

51 Acknowledge the receipt: ibid

68 On April 5 he sent: ibid 392

68 The truth is that: ibid, ORA S1, V1, 245

69 Simon Cameron: *Abraham Lincoln, a History* John Nicolay and John Hay, New York, 1890, IV 40

69 The expedition will go forward: Crawford 382

69 Shock left him dazed: LTC223, ORA S1, V1, 294

73 Navy steamers Powhatan: Welles

76 Inaugurate civil war: LTC251, ORN S1, V4, 249

78 The news of the fall: Perkins 716

78 We are to have civil war: ibid 711

79 The blind or mad politicians: ibid 706

100 He has proclaimed: *New York World* 7 January 1863

100 There seems to be no: ACT251, quoting Earl John Russell, 1863

100 What reason is there: Lincoln speech, 15 SEP 1862

101 Offer mediation: ACT253

103 In an instant twelve: ibid 254 quoting Allison

110 Elections took place: *History of the Civil War*, James Rhodes, MacMillan Co., New York, 1917 V4, 163

56125086R00081

Made in the USA
Lexington, KY
13 October 2016